The Diabetic Cookbook

365 Days of Diabetic friendly Easy to Cook Recipes

K.M. KASSI

© Copyright 2014 by K.M. KASSI - All rights reserved.

This document is geared towards providing exact and reliable information in regards to the topic and issue covered. The publication is sold with the idea that the publisher is not required to render accounting, officially permitted, or otherwise, qualified services. If advice is necessary, legal or professional, a practiced individual in the profession should be ordered.

- From a Declaration of Principles which was accepted and approved equally by a Committee of the American Bar Association and a Committee of Publishers and Associations.

In no way is it legal to reproduce, duplicate, or transmit any part of this document in either electronic means or in printed format. Recording of this publication is strictly prohibited and any storage of this document is not allowed unless with written permission from the publisher. All rights reserved.

The information provided herein is stated to be truthful and consistent, in that any liability, in terms of inattention or otherwise, by any usage or abuse of any policies, processes, or directions contained within is the solitary and utter responsibility of the recipient reader. Under no circumstances will any legal responsibility or blame be held against the publisher for any reparation, damages, or monetary loss due to the information herein, either directly or indirectly.

Respective authors own all copyrights not held by the publisher.

The information herein is offered for informational purposes solely, and is universal as so. The presentation of the information is without contract or any type of guarantee assurance.

The trademarks that are used are without any consent, and the publication of the trademark is without permission or backing by the trademark owner. All trademarks and brands within this book are for clarifying purposes only and are the owned by the owners themselves, not affiliated with this document.

Table of Content

Introduction i

Chapter 1 : Diabetic Cooking, Keep It Simple 1

Chapter 2 : A to Z of Food to Consume Raw or
Lightly Cooked 7

Chapter 3 : Breakfast Options 49

    Asparagus in Poached Egg 49

    Blueberry Pecan Parfait (Meal Replacement) 51

    Cantaloupe Smoothie (Meal Replacement) 52

    Dandelion Tisane (Coffee Substitute) 53

    Eggplant Omelet 55

    Feta and Cashew in Tomato Cups 56

    Garlic and Tomato Bruschetta 57

    Ham and Egg Cups 58

    Indigo Colored White Tea (Coffee Substitute) 60

    Jicama Bites 61

    Kiwi and Grapefruit Cold Brew (Meal Replacement) 62

    Lychee in Apple Juice (Meal Replacement) 63

    Mango and Berries in Steel-Cut Oats 64

    Nutty, Seedy Homemade Granola Bars 65

    Orange Zested, Banana Flavored Flapjacks 68

    Plantain Strips 69

    Quick ABC Oats (Apple, Berries, and Cashew) 70

    Raspberry and Pineapple Smoothie (Dairy-Free) 72

    Sardines on Flat Bread (No Cook) 73

    Toasted Strawberry and Cheese Sandwich 75

    Upland Cress and Avocado Open-Faced Sandwich 76

Viennoiseries: Easy Apple Turnover 78

Watermelon and Berry Slurry (Meal Replacement) 80

Xigua and Cucumber Slurry (Meal Replacement) 81

Yam with Coconut Butter 82

Zucchini Bruschetta 84

Chapter 4 : Lunch Recipes 85

Avocado and Steak Stuffed Pita Bread 85

Broccoli and Blue Cheese Salad 88

Chicken Salad on Toast 89

Devilled Eggs (Mayo Free, Spicy) 91

Endive Salad with Apples, Nuts and Cheese 93

Frozen Yogurt with Fruits (Meal Replacement) 95

Garlic Bread with Sweet Ham and Cheese 96

Halibut with French Beans and Peas 98

Iceberg Lettuce Wedge Salad with Mushrooms 100

Jerusalem Artichoke with Quail Eggs 102

Kale and Almonds on *Fusilli* 104

Lemony and Buttery Shrimp Rice 106

Macaroni and Chicken Fruit Cocktail Salad 108

Nectarine, Apple and Mint Cold Brew (Meal Replacement) 110

Olive Stuffed Kaiser Roll 111

Parmesan Crusted Tilapia 113

Quinoa with Herbs and Nuts 114

Reuben Sandwich (Low Fat) 115

Smoked Salmon and Herbed Cream Cheese Sandwich 117

Three-Cheese Salad on Fresh Greens 118

Uccelli Scappati (Rolled Veal) 120

Valencia Salad (*Ensalada Valencia*) 122

Watercress Salad with Cucumbers and Smoked Salmon 124
Xacuti 127
Yang Chow 130
Zesty Pork Tenderloin with Wild Rice 132

Chapter 5 : Dinner in 6 Steps (or Fewer) 133
Acquacotta (Slow Cooker Recipe) 133
Beef Bourguignon 135
Chili: Meaty, Spicy, Speedy (Slow Cooker Recipe) 137
Daikon, Pork and Taro in Stewed Tamarind
(Slow Cooker Recipe) 139
Egg Drop Soup with Straw Mushrooms 141
Fennel, Caper and Peas on Baked Snapper 142
Grapes and Stir-Fried Pork Tenderloin 144
Hot Halibut with Pineapples and Peppers 146
Inferno Chicken-Ginger Stew 147
Jalapeño Chicken Fillets 148
Kick Ass Cheesy Beef and Mushroom Slider 150
Laing (Taro Leaves in Coconut Sauce, Slow Cooker Recipe) ... 152
Mushroom Stew (Slow Cooker Recipe, Vegan) 153
Nimbu Rice: Spiced Rice with Cashew and Chili (Vegan) 155
Olive and Cheese Bruschetta with Smoked Salmon 157
Prawns in Buttery Garlic Rice 158
Quaglie con Pancetta (Quail Wrapped Pancetta) 160
Ragu with Lentils (Slow Cooker Recipe) 162
Sopas (Creamy Soup, Slow Cooker Recipe) 163
Tangy Sugar-Free Cola Chicken 164
Urta con Verduras: Bream with Vegetables 166
Vegetable, Chicken and Mushroom Pot Pie 168

Waldorf Salad with Cashew Nuts 170
Xia (Shrimps) Tangerine Stew with Swamp Cabbage 172
Yin-Yang Beef with Vegetables 174
Zesty Shrimps and Tofu with French Beans 176

Chapter 6 : Cold Infusions: Snacks and Meal Replacements 178
Black Tea with Cinnamon and Blackberries........................... 178
Black Tea with Blood Oranges and Mint 178
Black Tea with Black Cherries and Lemon Balm Flowers 180
Black Tea with Black Raspberries and Lavender Flowers......... 181
Black Tea with Black Mulberries, Red Grapes and
Fennel Seeds 182
Black Tea with Black Mulberries, Red Grapes and
Fennel Seeds 183
Green Tea with Basil and Strawberries 184
Green Tea with Berries 185
Green Tea with Tart Green Mangoes and Cucumbers 186
Green Tea with Blueberries, Lemon and Lime...................... 187
Green Tea with Ripe Mango and Sweet Orange.................... 188
Green Tea with Citrus 189
Green Tea with Fruit Seeds 190
Green Tea with Lemon and Spinach Leaves......................... 191
Green Tea with Arugula Leaves, Lime, and Kale Leaves 192
White Tea with Peaches and Mint.. 193
White Tea with Spiced Apples and Oranges 194
White Tea with Apples and Watermelon.............................. 195
Satsuma Infusion 196
Cilantro and Lemon Infusion... 197
Cilantro, Cucumber, and Lemon Infusion............................ 198

Orange Peel and Grape Infusion 199
Strawberries and Elderberry Flowers Infusion 200
Apricot, Nectarine and Peach Infusion 201
Large Citrus Infusion 202
Small Citrus Infusion 203
Peaches and Thyme Infusion 204
Grapefruit and Rosemary Infusion 205
Grape, Lemon, Strawberry and Thyme Infusion 206
Watermelon and Raspberry Infusion 207
Tropical Fruit Infusion 208
Blueberry, Kiwi Fruit, and Raspberry Infusion 209

Conclusion 210

Introduction

I want to thank you and congratulate you for downloading the book, **"365 Days of Diabetic Friendly Easy to Cook Recipes."**

Diabetes mellitus, or simply diabetes is a lifelong condition with chronic symptoms that affects the body's ability to process nutrients in food. This is due to insulin imbalance in the bloodstream. Type I diabetics do not produce enough insulin hormone, which causes cells to ignore/reject nutrients from food. This causes the person to lose weight due to malnutrition. Type II diabetics produce too much insulin, which causes cells to go on hyper drive, demanding more nutrients without properly processing these out of the body. This causes the person to gain a lot of weight.

Other types of diabetes (e.g. gestational, geriatric, pregnancy-related, etc.) switch irregularly from insulin resistance to insulin sensitivity. This leads to: permanent/irreversible damage to the eyes, heart, kidneys and the nervous system. People with diabetes have higher risks of blindness, cardiovascular ailments, kidney diseases, nerve damage, and stroke.

Fortunately, some symptoms can be managed by making minor adjustments in one's diet.

This book contains tips on how to control insulin sensitivity without the need for food supplements, medications or invasive surgeries. This can be achieved by preparing meals lightly, eating whole foods (unprocessed,) and keeping meals simple. Of course, it helps greatly to create sugar-free/unsweetened meals or choose dishes low in simple carbohydrates to prevent insulin imbalance.

This book contains recipes that should easily tide you over for the next 365 days.

Thanks again for downloading this book, I hope you enjoy it!

CHAPTER 1
Diabetic Cooking, Keep It Simple

Although many health care providers recommend the use of medications to treat symptoms of diabetes, this often becomes a costly affair in the long run, with medicine bills running up to several thousands of dollars in a year. Operations like bariatric surgeries are too invasive and expensive. Consuming commercially produced food supplements are pricey, inefficient, and potentially dangerous especially when combined with other medications, and without the approval of health care providers.

By cooking your own meals, and keeping things simple, you can prevent or lessen some of the more problematic symptoms of diabetes. Here are a few more things to keep in mind:

1. **<u>Avoid or severely limit consuming all forms of sweeteners.</u>**
   Consuming sweets (in all its forms) is the primary reason why sugar in the bloodstream spikes (too much) and crashes (not enough.) This is especially dangerous for Type II diabetics whose cells are already on hyper drive. Consuming even the smallest amount of sugar can make them crave for more sweets. The more sweets they eat, the more intense their cravings become. This cycle can last a long time if the person doesn't physically force himself/herself to stop eating.

   Not only does this lead to uncontrollable weight gain, but it also increases risk of heart attacks, gastrointestinal diseases, kidney failure, and stroke.

If possible, avoid consuming all forms of sweeteners, both organic and artificial. These include: *acesulfame potassium, advantame, aspartame,* brown sugar, *cyclamate,* date sugar, fructose, *galactose,* glucose, honey, jiggery, *lactose* (found in milk,) *maltodextrins, maltose,* molasses, *muscovado, noetame,* palm sugar, powdered sugar (confectioners' sugar,) raw sugar, saccharin, *sorbitol, sucralose,* sucrose, sugar cane sugar, unrefined sugar, white refined, sugar, *xylitol,* etc.

Avoid consuming any product (baked goods, beer, colas, confections, energy drinks, etc.) that contain these as well.

If you must, use only small amounts of green *stevia*. This product *least* affects blood sugar levels, but must not be taken in huge volumes. Or, if sugar consumption is unavoidable, eat only the smallest portions.

2. **Avoid or severely limit consuming simple carbohydrates.**
Sugar and all forms of sweeteners are processed by the body as simple carbohydrates. These are not necessarily bad for one's health. In fact, simple carbs are quickly converted into glucose, which is the brain's primary source of nutrient.

This becomes problematic when the person consumes too much, and the brain and/or body cannot process these properly anymore. Unfortunately, the body has a tendency to hoard glucose, which is considered "essential" when the body is under stress.

When there is too much glucose in the bloodstream, the body immediately converts these into *joules* (calories,) and then produces fat cells (adipose tissues,) where it hoards excess amounts. This leads to steady weight gain, and is visibly manifested in the expanding size of a person's midsection, calves, upper back area, and under the arms where adipose tissues are most abundant.

Because glucose is considered essential to the brain's survival, the body releases its supply of stored calories in the slowest possible manner. This is the reason why it is hard to lose weight in the first place.

Glucose is also a form of sugar which adversely affects diabetics' insulin level.

If possible, avoid or severely limit your simple carbohydrate intake. These can be found in:

- Sugars and sweeteners, all kinds
- Overly refined flour and grains, e.g. white flour, white rice, instant/quick-cooking oats, instant/quick-cooking couscous, etc. Avoid products that contain these as well, such ready-made cake/dough mixes, and commercially produced baked goods, bread, cookies, pastries, etc.
- Processed food, all kinds
- Processed or commercially produced drinks and beverages, all kinds

3. **<u>Limit consumption of food items rich in fat and oils.</u>**
Again, fat and oils are technically not bad for one's health. These are essential in keeping hair and nails looking shiny, and for keeping skin looking young.

Overconsumption can delay digestion and nutrient absorption. For diabetics, who already have compromised nutrient absorption capabilities, this becomes a bigger problem.

For Type I diabetics, this can lead to the first stages of malnutrition (the body does not gain enough calories, vitamins, and minerals to sustain good health even after eating large meals.) When untreated, this leads to weight loss, permanent inability to process food, organ failure, and diabetic coma.

For Type II diabetics, this could lead to more weight gain, and compromised internal organs too due to fatty buildup. They have higher chances of having a heart attack or stroke.

Whenever possible, choose cooking methods that use the least amount of oil, like: steaming, boiling, broiling, and frying on dry (no oil) pans. Use leaner cuts of meat, and limit the use of store-bought products with high oil content, like: butter, margarine, commercial salad dressings, baked goods, pre-marinated meat/frozen dinners, etc.

4. **Avoid or severely limit the use of processed food**.
Most processed food and drinks are created for the sake of convenience and profit, rather than for good health and flavor. Many food manufacturers use simple carbohydrates like overly refined flour and sugar, to stretch out their products. This brings production costs down and increases profits.

Others use oil and salt as flavoring agents and preservatives. And then there are those who use artificial/man-made, chemical-based food additives that cause all manner of health issues (e.g. cancer, thyroid dysfunction, gastrointestinal ulcers, etc.)

To ensure that you don't suffer from insulin imbalance (and other complications) avoid consuming processed food. Use fresh produce every time. If unavoidable, use processed food as sparingly as possible.

5. **Stick to recommended portions when eating.**
   One common mistake diabetics make is: consuming healthy or diabetic-approved ingredients/meals in large volumes. Anything in excess is bad for one's health. This is particularly true if you are trying to balance your blood sugar or insulin level.

Look at it this way: consuming 1 apple in the morning is good for you. Consuming 20 apples in one sitting everyday can cause multiple health issues.

This example seems absurd, but can you think back exactly how many cups of "healthy" green tea you have consumed today? Is it over the recommended serving size of 1 standard cup per meal, or a maximum of 5 cups a day?*

Quinoa is a great alternative to overly refined white rice, but are you consuming more than ½ (loosely packed) cup per meal, or a maximum of 1 cup a day?

Green *stevia* is a good substitute for table sugar. Are you consuming more than its recommended portion size of ½ tsp. per meal/drink, or a maximum of 2½ teaspoons a day.

If so, you need to rein in your consumption of "diabetic-friendly" food, drinks, or ingredients.

CHAPTER 2

A to Z of Food to Consume Raw or Lightly Cooked

A

1.

Acorn squash, cooked well
½ cup per meal
Maximum of 1 cup per day

2.

Acorn squash puree,
½ cup per meal
Maximum of ½ cup per day

3.

Adzuki beans, well coated
¼ cup per meal
Max ½ cup per day

4.

Alfalfa sprouts, fresh or lightly cooked
1 cup per meal
Max of 1 cup per day

5.

Almonds, roasted

¼ cup per meal
Max of ½ cup per day

6.

Apple, fresh or light cooked
1 medium piece, or 1 heaping cup per meal
Max of 3 pieces per day

7.

Apricot, fresh or lightly cooked
1 medium piece, or 1 heaping cup per meal
Max of 2 pieces per day

8.

Arborio rice, cooked
½ cup per meal
Max of 1½ cups per day

9.

Artichoke, lightly cooked
½ medium piece, approximately ¾ cup per meal
Max of ¾ cup per day

10.

Artichoke hearts, lightly cooked
2 medium pieces, approximately ½ cup per meal
Max of ½ cup per day

11.

Arugula, fresh
1 heaping cup per meal
2 heaping cups per day

12.

Asparagus, lightly cooked
1 heaping cup per meal
Max of 2 heaping cups per day

13.

Aubergine, lightly cooked
1 small piece 4 to 6 inches long or 1 cup per meal
Max of 1 small piece or 1 cup per day

14.

Avocado, fresh or lightly cooked
½ medium piece per meal
Max of 1 piece per day

B

15.

Bamboo shoots, lightly cooked
1 small piece, approximately 1 cup per meal
Max of 1 cup per day

16.
Banana, ripe or slightly unripe, fresh or lightly cooked
1 medium piece, approximately 6 to 8 inches long or 1 heaping cup per meal
Max of 3 pieces per day

17.
Banana blossoms, well cooked
½ cup per meal
Max of ½ cup per meal

18.
Basmati rice, see **Arborio rice**

19.
Bean sprouts, raw or lightly cooked
½ loosely packed cup per meal
Max of 1 cup per day

20.
Bell pepper, raw or lightly cooked
½ large piece, approximately ¾ cup per meal
Max of 2½ cups per day

21.
Beet greens, lightly cooked
½ heaping cup per meal
Max of 1 cup per day

22.

Beet roots, raw or boiled / stewed
1 large piece (approximately 2 small pieces,) approximately ¾ cups per meal
Max ¾ cups per day

23.

Bhutanese red rice, see **Arborio rice**

24.

Bitter gourd, cooked well
1 medium piece approximately 6 to 8 inches long, or 1 heaping cup per meal
Max of 1 heaping cup per day

25.

Blackberries, fresh or lightly cooked
½ cup per meal
Max of 1 cup per day

26.

Black / red / white currants, see **Blackberries**

27.

Black-eyed peas, see **Adzuki beans**

28.

Black *Japonica* rice, see **Arborio rice**

29.

Blueberries, see **Blackberries**

30.

Blood orange, peeled, fresh
1 medium piece or 1 cup of loosely packed orange pulp per meal
Max of 2 pieces per day

31.

Blood orange juice, freshly squeezed
1 cup per meal
Max of 2 cups per day

32.

Bok Choy, lightly cooked
2 large heads, or 1½ cups per meal
Max of 3 cups per day

33.

Boston lettuce (butter head), fresh with little or no dressing
1 medium head, or approximately 2 heaping cups per meal
4 cups per day

34.

Brazil nuts, shelled, well roasted
2 pieces per day
Max of 2 pieces per day

35.

Breadfruit, unripe, cooked well
¾ cup per meal
Max of ¾ cup per day

36.

Broccoli, lightly cooked
1 medium head with leaves, stalks and stems, approximately 2 cups, 1 heaping cup per meal
Max of 2 cups per day

37.

Brown rice, see **Arborio rice**

38.

Brussels sprouts, lightly cooked
1½ heaping cups per meal
Max of 1½ heaping cups per day

39.

Butternut squash, see **Acorn squash**

C

40.

Cabbage, raw, shredded (e.g. coleslaw)
½ small head or ¾ cup packed per meal
Max of ¾ cup packed per day

41.

Cabbage, lightly cooked
1 small head or 1 cup packed per meal
Max of 2 cups packed per day

42.

Caimito, fresh
1 medium piece per meal
Max of 2 pieces per day

43.

Calabaza squash, see **Acorn squash**

44.

Calamondin juice, freshly made, unsweetened
8 large pieces or approximately ¾ cup per meal
Max of ¾ cup per day

45.

Carrot, raw
1 medium piece or ½ cup per meal
Max of 2 medium pieces, or 1 cup per day

46.

Carrot, lightly cooked
¾ cup per meal
Max of 2½ cups per day

47.

Carrot juice, freshly squeezed
1 cup per meal
Max of 2 cups per day

48.

Cashew apple, fresh
1 medium piece per meal
Max of 1 piece per day

49.

Cashew apple juice, freshly made, unsweetened
¾ cup per meal
Max of ¾ cup per day

50.

Cashew nuts, roasted
¼ cup per meal

Max of ¾ cup per day

51.

Cassava or *yucca*, cooked well
½ small piece or ¾ cup per meal
Max of ¾ cup per meal

52.

Cauliflower, lightly cooked
1 small head or 1½ loosely packed cup per meal
Max of 1½ cup per day

53.

Celeriac or celery root, fresh or lightly cooked
⅛ small piece, or ½ cup per meal
Max of ½ cup per day

54.

Celery, fresh or lightly cooked
1 medium stalk, strings removed, approximately ½ cup per meal
Max of 1½ cups per day

55.

Chayote, cooked well
2 small pieces or 1½ heaping cups per meal
Max of 1½ cups per day

56.

Cherimoya, fresh
1 medium piece per meal
Max of 1 piece per day

57.

Cherries, fresh, or lightly prepared
½ cup per meal
Max of 1 cup per day

58.

Chestnuts, shelled, roasted
½ cup per meal
Max of 1 cup per day

59.

Chickpeas (garbanzos,) see **Adzuki beans**

60.

Chinese spinach, lightly cooked
1 cup per meal
Max of 2 cups per day

61.

Clementine, fresh
2 medium pieces per meal
Max of 4 medium pieces per day

62.

Cloudberries, see **Blackberries**

63.

Collard greens, stems and leaves, lightly cooked
1 cup per meal
Max of 2 cups per day

64.

Coconut, dried/desiccated
¼ cup per meal
Max of ¼ cup per day

65.

Coconut flesh, fresh or lightly cooked
½ cup per meal
Max of ½ cup per day

66.

Coconut juice or fresh coconut milk
1 cup per meal
Max of 2 cups per day

67.

Corn, baby, lightly cooked
6 to 8 pieces or approximately ¾ cup per meal
Max of ¾ cup per day

69.

Corn on cob, lightly cooked
1 small piece 4 to 5 inches long per meal
Max of 1 piece per day

70.

Corn kernels, whole, lightly cooked
½ cup per meal
Max 1 cup per day

71.

Corn, freshly creamed, baked/ stewed
½ cup per meal
Max ½ cup per day

72.

Cucumber, fresh
1 medium piece, approximately 6 to 8 inches long or 1½ cups per meal
Max of 3 pieces per day

73.

Chia seeds, roasted
1 ounce per day, approximately 6 level teaspoons per meal
Max of 6 teaspoons a day

74.

Chickpeas, well cooked

½ cup per day
Max of 1 cup per day

75.

Cranberries, see **Blueberries**

76.

Cranberry juice
1 cup per meal
Max of 1 cup per day

77.

Custard apple, fresh
1 medium piece, approximately ¾ cup per meal
Max of 1 piece per day

D

78.

Daikon or Asian radish, lightly cooked
1 large piece, approximately 8 to 10 inches long, or 2 heaping cups per meal
Max of 1 large piece per day

79.

Daikon or Asian radish, lightly pickled
1 large piece, approximately 8 to 10 inches long, or 2 heaping cups per meal
Max of 2 large pieces per day

80.

Delicata squash, see **Acorn squash**

81.

Dragon fruit or *pitaya*, fresh
1 medium piece, approximately ¾ cup per meal
Max of ¾ cup per day

82.

Durian, ripe, fresh
¼ cup per meal
Max of ¼ cup per day

83.

Durian coffee, freshly made
½ cup per meal
Max of ½ cup per day

E

84.

Egg, lightly cooked
1 large piece per meal
Max of 1 piece per day

85.

Egg yolk, raw or lightly cooked
2 large pieces per meal

Max of 2 pieces per day

86.

Eggplant, see **Aubergine**

87.

Endive, fresh or lightly cooked
1 small head, approximately 1 heaping cup per meal
Max of 1 small head per day

F

88.

Fava beans (broad beans,) see **Adzuki beans**

89.

Fennel, raw or lightly cooked
¼ small piece or ½ cup per meal
Max of 1 cup per day

90.

Fiddleheads, lightly cooked
1 cup per meal
Max of 1 cup per day

91.

Figs, raw or lightly cooked
3 medium pieces
Max of 3 medium pieces per day

92.

Flax seeds, see **Chia seeds**

93.

French beans, lightly cooked
½ cup per meal
Max of ½ cup per day

G

94.

Grapes, raw
¾ cup per meal
Max of 2½ cups per day

95.

Green beans, see **French Beans**

96.

Green leaf lettuce or red leaf lettuce, see **Boston lettuce**

97.

Grapefruit, fresh
¼ large piece or 1 heaping cup per meal
Max of 1 cup per day

98.

Grapefruit juice, fresh
¼ large piece or 1 heaping cup per meal
2 cups per day

99.

Gooseberries, see **Blackberries**

100.

Guava, fresh or cooked well
3 medium pieces per meal
Max of 3 pieces per day

H

101.

Hazelnuts, shelled, roasted
½ cup per meal
Max of ½ per day

102.

Honeydew melon, fresh
1 heaping cup per meal
Max of 1 cup per day

103.

Honeydew melon juice, freshly made, unsweetened
1 cup per meal
Max of 2 cups per meal

104.

Hubbarb squash, see **Acorn squash**

I

105.

Iceberg lettuce, fresh
1 small head approximately 2 heaping cups per meal
Max of 2 small heads per day

106.

Ivy gourd, see **Bitter gourd**

J

107.

Jackfruit, unripe, shredded, cooked well
1/8 medium-sized fruit, approximately 1 cup per meal
Max of 1 cup per day

108.

Jackfruit, ripe
50 grams of jackfruit pulp, approximately 1/4 cup per meal
Max of 1/2 cup per day

109.

Japanese persimmon (Asian persimmon, kaki persimmon, Sharon fruit,) fresh
1 medium piece per meal

Max of 1 piece per day

110.

Jasmine rice, see **Arborio rice**

111.

Jerusalem artichoke
1 small knob, approximately ½ cup per meal
Max of 1 small knob per day

112.

Jicama, raw or lightly pickled
¼ small piece, approximately ½ cup per meal
Max of 1 cup per day

K

113.

Kabocha squash, see **Acorn squash**

114.

Kaffir lime, fresh
2 large pieces, approximately ½ cup of pulp per meal
Max of 4 large pieces per day

115.

Kaffir lime juice, fresh, unsweetened
1 cup per meal
Max of 1 cup per day

116.

Kale, lightly cooked
1 cup per meal
Max of 2 cups per day

117.

Key lime, see **Kaffir lime**

118.

Kiwi fruit, fresh or lightly cooked
2 large pieces, approximately ¾ cup per meal
Max of 2 large pieces per day

119.

Kumquat, fresh
2 medium pieces, approximately ¾ cup per meal
Max of 2 pieces per day

L

120.

Lanzones, fresh
2 heaping cups per meal
Max of 4 heaping cups per day

121.

Lemon, fresh, peeled
1 medium piece or ¾ cup of lemon pulp per meal
Max of 3 whole fruits per day

122.

Lemon juice, freshly squeezed
1 cup per meal
Max of 3 cups per day

123.

Lentils, see **Adzuki beans**

124.

Lima beans, see **Adzuki beans**

125.

Lime, fresh, peeled
2 medium pieces or 1 cup of lime pulp per meal
Max of 4 whole fruits per day

126.

Limequats, see ***Calamondin***

127.

Loganberries, see **Blackberries**

128.

Longan fruits, see *Lanzones*

129.

Long grain rice, see **Arborio rice**

130.

Loquats, see **Kumquats**

131.

Lotus root, cooked well
½ cup per meal
Max of ½ cup per day

132.

Lychee, see *Lanzones*

M

133.

Mabolo, see **Japanese persimmon**

134.

Macadamia nuts, see **Brazil nuts**

135.

Mango, ripe, fresh
1 cheek from medium-sized fruit
Max of 2 cheeks or 1 whole mango per day

136.

Mango, unripe, fresh
1 cheek from medium-sized fruit
Max of 1 cheek per day

137.

Mango juice, ripe, fresh, unsweetened
1 cup approximately 1 medium-sized fruit
Max of 1 cup per day

138.

Mango juice, unripe, fresh, with ½ tsp. sweetener
½ cup approximately 1 mango cheek
Max of ½ cup per day

139.

Mangosteen, ripe
4 large pieces per meal
Max of 4 large pieces per day

140.

Marang, see **Durian**

141.

Medium grain rice, see **Arborio rice**

142.

Melon, fresh
1 heaping cup per meal
Max of 1 cup per day

143.

Melon juice, freshly made, unsweetened
1 cup per meal
Max of 1 cup per day

144.

Mizuna (California peppergrass, Japanese greens, spider mustard,) fresh
½ packed cup per meal
Max of 2 cups per day

145.

Mulberries, see **Blackberries**

146.

Mung beans, see **Adzuki beans**

147.

Mung sprouts, fresh or lightly cooked

1 cup heaping per meal
Max of 1 cup per day

148.

Mushrooms, fresh, lightly cooked
½ cup per meal
Max of 2 cups per day

149.

Mushrooms, dried, cooked well
½ cup per meal
Max of 2 cups per day

150.

Muskmelon, see **Melon**

151.

Mustard greens, fresh or lightly cooked
½ cup per meal
Max of 1 cup per day

N

152.

Napa cabbage, raw or lightly cooked
2 large leaves or approximately ½ cup per meal
Max of 1 cup per day

153.

Native currants, see **Black currants**

154.

Nectarine, raw
1 small piece, ¾ cup per meal
Max of ¾ cups per day

O

155.

Oats, steel cut or Irish oatmeal, cooked well
(Do not use instant or quick cooking oats as these are already overly-refined, and commercial blends usually have artificial flavors and sweeteners.)
½ cup per meal, lightly seasoned, dairy-free
Max of 1 cup per cup

156.

Okra, lightly cooked
1 cup per meal
Max of 2 cups per day

157.

Orange, see **Blood orange**

158.

Orange juice, see **Blood orange juice**

P

159.

Papaya, ripe
1½ cups per meal
Max of 3 cups per day

160.

Papaya, unripe, cooked well
½ cup per meal
Max of 1 cup per day

161.

Papaya juice, ripe, freshly made, unsweetened
1 cup per meal
Max of 1 cup per day

162.

Parsnip, lightly cooked
1 small piece or approximately 1 cup per meal
Max 1 cup per day

163.

Passion fruit, fresh
1 large piece or approximately ¼ cup of passion fruit seeds per meal
Max of ½ cup per day

164.

Peas, green / frozen, lightly cooked
½ cup per meal
Max of 1 cup per day

165.

Peach, see **Apricot**

166.

Peanut butter fruits, see **Figs**

167.

Peanuts, unshelled, boiled
1 cup per meal
Max of 1 cup per day

168.

Peanuts, shelled, roasted / cooked well
¼ cup per meal
Max of ½ cup per day

169.

Pear, fresh or lightly cooked
1 medium piece or approximately ¾ cups per meal
Max of 1 piece per day

170.

Pecan nuts, see **Almonds**

171.

Pili nuts, see **Brazil nuts**

172.

Pineapple, fresh
¼ medium piece or approximately 1 cup per meal
Max of 3 cups per day

173.

Pineapple, canned in light syrup
¼ cup per meal
Max of ½ cup per day

174.

Pineapple juice, made from fresh fruit
1 cup per meal
Max of 3 cups a day

175.

Pine nuts, see **Almonds**

176.

Pistachio nuts, see **Almonds**

177.

Plantain, see **Banana**

178.

Plum, fresh or lightly cooked
2 medium pieces per meal
Max of 2 pieces per day

179.

Pomegranate, fresh
1 large piece per meal
Max of 2 large pieces per day

180.

Pomegranate juice, fresh
1 cup per meal
Max of 2 cups per day

181.

Pomelo, see **Grapefruit**

182.

Potato, cooked well
1 medium piece, approximately ½ cup per meal
Max of 1 cup per day

183.
Purple sticky rice, see **Arborio rice**

184.
Purple *granadilla*, see **Passion fruit**

185.
Prickly fruit flower, fresh
4 to 6 medium pieces, approximately ¾ cup per meal
Max of ¾ cup per day

186.
Prune, dried, pitted
2 large pieces or approximately ¼ cup per meal
Max of ¼ cup per day

187.
Prune juice, unsweetened
¾ cup per meal
Max of ¾ cup per day

188.
Pumpkin, well cooked
¾ cup per meal
Max ¾ cups per day

189.
Pumpkin juice, unsweetened
¾ cup per meal
Max ¾ cups per day

190.
Pumpkin puree, well cooked
¾ cup per meal
Max ¾ cups per day

191.
Pumpkin seeds, roasted
¼ cup per meal
Max of ½ cup per day

192.
Pomegranate, fresh, seeds only
1 medium piece or ½ cup per meal
Max 1 piece per day

193.
Pomegranate juice
¾ cup per meal
Max ¾ cup per day

Q

194.
Quandong, see **Apricot**

195.
Quince, fresh
1 medium piece or 1 cup per meal
Maximum of 1 cup per day

196.
Quinoa, cooked well
½ cup cooked per meal
Maximum of 1 cup per day

R

197.
Radicchio, see **Endive**

198.
Radish, fresh or lightly cooked
4 small pieces or ½ cup per meal
Max of ½ cup per day

199.
Raisins, dried
¼ cup per meal
Max of ½ cup per day

200.

Rambutan, fresh
1 heaping cup per meal
Max of 1 cup per day

201.

Raspberries, see **Blueberries**

202.

Rhubarb, fresh
1 cup per meal
Maximum of 1 cup per day

203.

Rhubarb, cooked well
½ cup per meal
Maximum of ½ cup per day

204.

Romaine lettuce, see **Boston lettuce**

205.

Rutabaga, see **Parsnip**

S

206.

Santol flesh, fresh
2 large pieces per day

Max of 2 pieces per day

207.

Santol seeds, fresh
½ cup per day
Max of ½ cup per day

208.

Satsuma, fresh
3 medium pieces or 1½ heaping cups of pulp per meal
Max of 3 medium pieces per day

209.

Sea beet, see **Collard greens**

210.

Sea kale stems, see **Asparagus**

211.

Sesame seeds, see **Chia seeds**

212.

Sea weeds, fresh (e.g. *Arame, Badderlocks, Carola, Dulse, Kombu, Laver, Nori, Ogonori, Wakame, Sea grape, Sea lettuce, etc.*)
½ heaping cup per meal
Max of 1 cup per day

213.

Sea weeds, dried (e.g. *Dulse, Kombu, Laver, Nori,* etc.)
¼ cup per meal
Max of ½ cup per day

214.

Short grain rice, see **Arborio rice**

215.

Snap beans, see **French Beans**

216.

Soy nuts, roasted
¼ cup per meal
Max ¾ cup per day

217.

Spaghetti squash, see **Acorn squash**

218.

Spinach leaves, cooked well
½ cup per meal
Max of 1 cup per day

219.

Spinach leaves (baby,) fresh
1 cup per meal

Max of 2 cups per day

230.

Squash flowers, lightly cooked
1 cup per meal
Max of 1 cup per meal

231.

Star apple, see *Caimito*

232.

Strawberries, fresh or lightly cooked
1 cup per meal
Max of 2 cups per day

233.

String beans, see **French Beans**

234.

Sugar apple, fresh
1 large piece per meal
Max of 1 piece per day

235.

Sunflower seeds, roasted
¼ cup per meal
Max of ¼ cup per day

236.

Sweet potato, cooked well
1 medium piece or 1 cup per meal
Max of 1 cup per day

237.

Swiss chard, see **Collard greens**

T

238.

Taro, see **Sweet Potato**

240.

Taro leaves, cooked well
1 packed cup per meal
Max of 1 cup per day

241.

Tomatoes, fresh or lightly cooked
2 large pieces, or 3 medium pieces, or 5 small pieces, 1 cup per meal
Max of 3 cups per day

242.

Turnip, see **Parsnip**

U

243.

Ugli fruit, fresh
1 small piece or 1 heaping, loosely packed cup of *ugli* flesh per meal
Max of 1 heaping cup per day

244.

Upland Cress, fresh
½ cup per meal
Max of 2 cups per day

V

245.

Victoria plums, fresh
3 small pieces or 1 cup per meal
Max of 1 cup per day

W

246.

Walnuts, roasted
¼ cup per meal
Max of ½ cup per day

247.

Water chestnuts, cooked well
4 medium pieces or ¼ cup per meal
Max of ¼ cup per day

248.
Watercress, see **Upland Cress**

249.
Watermelon, fresh
⅛ wedge or 2 heaping cups of watermelon flesh per meal
Max of 4 cups per day

250.
Watermelon seeds, roasted
¼ cup per meal
Max of ½ cup per day

251.
Water spinach, see **Chinese spinach**

252.
Wax beans, see **French Beans**

253.
Whortleberry or bilberry, see **Blackberries**

254.
Wild rice, see **Arborio rice**

255.

Winged beans, see **French Beans**

X

256.

Xigua or golden watermelon , see **Watermelon**

Y

257.

Yam, boiled or stewed
1 small piece or ½ cup per meal
1 cup per day

Z

258.

Zucchini, fresh or lightly blanched
1 medium piece or 1 heaping cup per meal
1 cup per day

259.

Zucchini flowers, see **Squash flowers**

Chapter 3

Breakfast Options

260.

Asparagus in Poached Egg

Makes 1 Serving

Ingredients:

1	piece, large	egg, at room temperature
4	spears, large	asparagus, tough ends snapped off, (add more if desired,) rinse well, drain
-	-	sea salt, to taste
-	-	water, for boiling

Directions:

1. Half-fill deep saucepan with water set over high heat. Add pinch of salt. Let water come to a rolling* boil.
2. Dunk asparagus spears in water. Cook until these turn a shade brighter, about 3 minutes. Remove from saucepan and drain on paper towels. Keep warm. Lightly season prior to serving.
3. Using a slotted spoon, gently lower egg into boiling water. Cook for only 4 minutes. Remove from pan immediately. Place on egg holder.

4. Slice top off. Egg should still be fluid inside.
5. <u>To serve</u>: place asparagus spears on small plate, and serve egg on the side. Dip asparagus into egg and eat while warm.

261

Blueberry Pecan Parfait (Meal Replacement)

Makes 1 Serving

Ingredients:

½	cup, level	cottage cheese, rinsed and drained well, chilled for 15 minutes before using
½	cup, heaping	frozen blueberries, thawed slightly
1	tsp., heaping	roasted pecan, unseasoned

Directions:

1. In a parfait glass (or any tall, glass container,) layer ingredients from the bottom up: frozen blueberries, cottage cheese, and pecans. Serve immediately.

262. Cantaloupe Smoothie (Meal Replacement)

Makes 1 Serving

Ingredients:

1	cup	very rip cantaloupe, deseeded, roughly chopped
½	cup	crushed ice
¼	cup	orange juice, freshly squeezed

Directions:

1. Place all ingredients into blender. Process until smooth. Serve immediately.

263. Dandelion Tisane (Coffee Substitute)

Makes 4 Servings
Recommended Serving size: 1 cup per person

Ingredients:

1	tsp., level	dried/powdered dandelion root
1	tsp., heaping	dandelion flowers
¼	tsp.	fennel seeds, lightly crushed with flat side of knife
¼	tsp.	fresh peppermint leaves, whole (or 1 peppermint teabag)
1	quart (4 cups)	freshly boiled water (212°F or 100°C)

Directions:

1. Place all ingredients into coffee or French press (or any large coffee/tea pot.) Steep ingredients for 5 to 10 minutes.
2. Strain tea while serving. Serve immediately.

Eggplant Omelet

Makes 1 Serving

Ingredients:

2	pieces, small	ripe cherry or grape tomatoes, quartered
1	piece, large	egg, whisked until frothy
1	piece, thick cut	bacon, roughly chopped
½	piece, small	eggplant, minced
2	tsp.	water
1	tsp.	cottage cheese, rinsed and drained well
-	-	seat salt and black pepper, to taste

Directions:

1. Place bacon and water in nonstick frying pan set over medium heat. Cook until water evaporates and bacon starts to crisp, about 3 minutes. Scrape bacon bits to 1 side of the pan.
2. Add in minced eggplants and stir-fry until golden.

3. Lower heat to lowest setting. Pour in whisked egg. Gently stir to combine all 3 ingredients. Put lid on. Cook until egg is set in the center, about 3 to 5 minutes.
4. Fold omelet in half and transfer to a plate. Spread cottage cheese on top. Dot with tomatoes. Season lightly with salt and pepper, if desired. Serve warm.

265. Feta and Cashew in Tomato Cups

Makes 1 Serving

Ingredients:

1	piece, large	ripe tomato, halved horizontally, deseeded
1	tsp.	roasted cashew nuts, lightly seasoned (don't use honey-roasted nuts), roughly chopped,
1	tsp.	feta cheese, crumbled
-	dash	black pepper

Directions:

1. Combine feta cheese and cashew nuts in a small bowl. Divide in 2 equal portions.
2. Spoon equal portions into prepared tomatoes. Season lightly with pepper. Serve.

200.

Garlic and Tomato Bruschetta

Makes 1 Serving

Ingredients:

2	slices, thick	sugar-free sourdough bread, toasted well on both sides
1	clove, large	garlic, peeled
2	tsp.	sun dried tomatoes in olive oil, minced
1	tsp.	reserve olive oil (from sun dried tomatoes)
1	tsp.	chives, minced

Directions:

Vigorously rub garlic clove on 1 side of each of the toasted bread slices

Spread equal portions of sun dried tomatoes on garlic side of bread. Sprinkle chives and drizzle olive oil on top.

Pop both slices into oven toaster, and cook until well heated through.

Place bruschetta on plate. Serve warm.

267.

Ham and Egg Cups

Makes 4 Servings
Recommended serving size: 1 cup per person

Ingredients:

8	pieces	quail eggs, fresh
4	slices	Canadian ham or sweet ham, sliced into wide slivers
1	slice, thick	sugar-free sourdough bread, quartered
2	tsp.	cheddar cheese, grated
-	-	white pepper, to taste

Directions:

1. Preheat oven to 350°F (175°F) for at least 10 minutes. Place 4 paper liners into large muffin tins. Set aside.
2. Place 1 bread quarter into base of each muffin cup. Break 2 quail eggs on top and sprinkle equal portions of cheese. Bake these for 10 to 15 minutes, or until eggs are set. Remove muffin tins from oven immediately.
3. Carefully remove each cup from muffin tins, and cool slightly for easier handling.
4. Season with pepper before serving. Serve warm.

268.
Indigo Colored White Tea (Coffee Substitute)

Makes 4 Servings
Recommended serving size: 1 cup per person

Ingredients:

1	quart (4 cups)	freshly boiled water (at 212°F or 100°C)
4	bags	white tea
1-2	piece(s)	chicory flowers
1-2	piece(s)	dayflower blossoms
1-2	piece(s)	porterweed blossoms
1	tsp.	green *stevia*, optional, divided

Directions:

1. Place white tea and freshly boiled water into coffee or French press (or any large coffee/tea pot.) Steep ingredients for 5 minutes.
2. Add in flowers. Steep for another 5 minutes. Strain tea while serving.
3. Stir in ¼ teaspoon green *stevia* per cup, if using. Serve immediately.

Note: always buy edible flowers from grocery stores or from vendors who specialize in salad flowers or candied flowers (for cakes and pastries.) Do not pick wild flowers, or use flowers from floral shops. These contain substances unfit for human consumption. Additionally, these blue flowers are bitter. You can lessen amount, or remove 1 or 2 blossoms off the recipe if you find it too unpalatable.

269.

Jicama Bites

Makes 1 Serving

Ingredients:

½	piece, small	*jicama* (also called Asian or Mexican turnip,) peeled, sliced into thick matchsticks, rinsed, drained well, chilled well before using
-	-	sea salt, to taste
½	tsp.	apple cider vinegar
½	tsp.	red pepper flakes, optional

Directions:

1. Combine salt, vinegar and red pepper flakes (if using,) until salt dissolves.
2. Drizzle on chilled *jicama*. Serve immediately.

270. Kiwi and Grapefruit Cold Brew (Meal Replacement)

Makes 2 Servings
Recommended serving size: 2 cups

Ingredients:		
2	pieces, large	kiwi fruits, peeled, quartered
1	piece, large	lemon, quartered, pips removed
1	piece, small	grapefruit, peeled, membranes and pips removed, torn into large chunks (substitute sweet *pomelo* if desired)
1	quart (4 cups)	filtered or spring water

Directions:

1. Combine ingredients in large, non-reactive pitcher. Put lid on. "Brew" beverage in fridge for 5 to 8 hours, stirring once every hour.
2. Strain brew before serving. Always serve chilled. You may eat the fruits, if desired.

271.

Lychee in Apple Juice (Meal Replacement)

Makes 1 Serving

Ingredients:

1	cup	organic apple juice, sugar-free / freshmade
¼	can, 15 Oz.	*lychee* in light syrup, rinsed well, drained, julienned

Directions:

1. Combine ingredients in large, non-reactive mug or container. Put lid on. "Brew" beverage in fridge for 1 to 2 hours.
2. Stir before serving. Always serve chilled. You may eat *lychee*, if desired.

272.

Mango and Berries in Steel-Cut Oats

Makes 1 Serving

Ingredients:

¼	cup	steel-cut oats (do not use instant or quick-cooking oats,) cooked according to package instructions, keep warm
1	piece, medium	mango cheek, ripe or slightly overripe, peeled, diced into bite-sized pieces
¼	cup, heaping	frozen blueberries

Directions:

1. Combine fresh cooked oats and frozen blueberries in a bowl. Mix well, mashing some berries as you go. Swirl oats to create a pretty pattern.
2. Add diced mangoes before serving. Serve warm.

273. Nutty, Seedy Homemade Granola Bars

Makes 10 Bars
Recommended Serving size: 1 bar per meal

Ingredients:		
1½	cup	steel cut oats, uncooked, toasted on dry pan until brown
½	cup	dried dates, pitted, minced, or pulsed in food processor until sticky
½	cup	almonds, raw, roughly chopped, toasted on dry pan until aromatic and golden
¼	cup	almond (or any nut) butter
2	Tbsp.	maple syrup
2	Tbsp.	chia seeds, raw, whole

2	Tbsp.	flax seeds, raw, whole
2	Tbsp.	sesame seeds, roasted on dry pan
2	Tbsp.	sunflower seeds, roasted, shelled

Directions:
1. Line 8"x8" deep dish with saran wrap. Set aside.
2. Combine granola ingredients in a bowl until well incorporated. Press mix into prepared dish. Cover with another layer of saran wrap. Flatten and press mix so that granola bars become dense and level. Chill in fridge for 15 to 30 minutes.
3. Remove mix from dish. Divide into 10 equal bars or squares. Serve.
4. Keep rest in freezer until ready to use.

274.
Orange Zested, Banana Flavored Flapjacks

Makes 1 Serving, about 2 Flapjacks

Ingredients:		
1	pieces, large	overripe bananas, mashed well
1	piece, small	egg, whisked until frothy
1	piece, small	orange, zested (reserve for later use,) juiced, strain to remove pips
¼	cup	whole grain flour
½	Tbsp.	coconut or grapeseed oil
½	tsp.	baking powder
-	pinch	sea salt
-	-	water, only if needed
-	-	oil, for grilling

Directions:

1. Combine ingredients in a large bowl. Whisk well to incorporate as much air into batter. If batter is too thick,

add water 1 tablespoon at a time until desired consistency is reached. Whisk well after each addition.
2. Heat pancake griddle or non-stick frying pan set over medium heat. Pour just enough oil to lightly grease cooking surface.
3. Pour half of the batter into hot pan. Cook until edges are set and center is bubbly. Do not press down on flapjacks or these will become dense and chewy. Flip once. Cook other side for another 1 to 2 minutes. Repeat step for remaining batter.
4. lapjacks. Serve plain or with more fresh bananas as garnish. Serve warm

275.

Plantain Strips

Makes 1 Serving

Ingredients:

2	pieces, large	plantain, ripe or overripe, peeled, sliced lengthwise into 4 wide strips each
½	Tbsp.	coconut oil, for frying

Directions:

1. Pour oil into non-stick pan set over medium heat. Fry plantain strips in hot oil until golden brown but not crisp.
2. Remove strips from hot oil. Place cooked plantains on plate lined with paper towel to drain excess grease. Serve immediately.

276.

Quick ABC Oats (Apple, Berries, and Cashew)

Makes 1 Serving

Ingredients:

¼	cup	steel-cut oats
¼	cup	blueberries, or any fresh berries
½	cup	milk, or any dairy-substitute (you can also use plain water)
½	piece, small	apple, cored, diced into bite-sized pieces
½	tsp., heaping	cashew nuts, lightly roasted, unseasoned, roughly chopped
½	tsp.	green *stevia*, optional

Directions:

1. Except for cashew nuts and *stevia*, combine remaining ingredients in a deep microwave-safe bowl. Stir.

2. Microwave on highest setting for 5 to 15 seconds. Keep a watchful eye on this. Stop cooking process before milk bubbles out of the bowl.
3. Carefully remove bowl from microwave. Cool slightly for easier handling.
4. Stir in *stevia* if using. Sprinkle cashew nuts on top. Serve warm.

277.
Raspberry and Pineapple Smoothie (Dairy-Free)

Makes 1 Serving

Ingredients:

1	can, 8 oz,	pineapple tidbits, rinsed well, drained
1	piece, small	overripe banana, roughly chopped
½	cup	frozen raspberries
½	cup	crushed ice

Directions:

1. Except for cashew nuts and *stevia*, combine remaining ingredients in a deep microwave-safe bowl. Stir.
2. Microwave on highest setting for 5 to 15 seconds. Keep a watchful eye on this. Stop cooking process before milk bubbles out of the bowl.
3. Carefully remove bowl from microwave. Cool slightly for easier handling.
4. Stir in *stevia* if using. Sprinkle cashew nuts on top. Serve warm.

Sardines on Flat Bread (No Cook)

Makes 4 Servings
Recommended Serving size: 1 quarter flat bread

Ingredients:		
4	pieces, small	buffalo mozzarella, drained well, torn
1	piece, 6-inch	sugar-free flatbread, warmed in skillet
1	piece, small	unripe (green) cherry tomato, deseeded, minced
1	handful, generous	arugula leaves, rinsed, spun-dried, add more if desired, roughly torn
½	can, 3.75 oz.	sardines in olive oil, reserve oil for drizzling
1	piece, small	lime, sliced into wedges, remove pips

| - | pinch, generous | red pepper flakes, optional |

Directions:

1. Place flatbread on large chopping board. Spread small amount of olive oil (from sardines) on top. Layer with arugula leaves. (Add as much as you want.)
2. Place sardines whole on top of leaves, or break these apart into smaller chunks.
3. Dot with torn mozzarella. Sprinkle minced tomatoes on top.
4. Divide flatbread into equal quarters. Serve with lime wedges.
5. Squeeze lime, and sprinkle with red pepper flakes (if using) before eating. Serve.

279.

Toasted Strawberry and Cheese Sandwich

Makes 1 Serving

Ingredients:

1	slice, thick	rye bread
1	tsp.	strawberry jam (any jam will do)
1	tsp., heaping	cottage cheese, rinsed and drained well
1	tsp., heaping	gouda cheese, shredded
½	tsp.	butter, for frying

Directions:

1. Spread jam on 1 side of bread. Slice in half diagonally.
2. Combine cheeses and spread on 1 bread slice. Top off with the other slice.
3. Place butter on non-stick frying pan set over medium heat.
4. Toast sandwich on both sides, about 3 minutes. Remove sandwich from pan.
5. Serve on plate with fresh berries. Serve warm.

280. Upland Cress and Avocado Open-Faced Sandwich

Makes 1 Serving

Ingredients:		
1	slice, thick	sugar-free pumpernickel bread, toasted
1	handful, generous	upland cress, thin stems and leaves only, add more if desired (substitute alfalfa sprouts, arugula leaves, or water cress)
½	piece, medium	avocado, pitted, peeled, coarsely mashed
1	tsp., heaping	Colby Jack cheese, grated
¼	tsp.	balsamic vinegar, for drizzling

Directions:

1. Spread mashed avocado on 1 side of bread. Place upland cress on top.
2. Drizzle balsamic vinegar before sprinkling cheese on top.
3. Heat open-faced sandwich in oven toaster until cheese melts.
4. Cool slightly before slicing. Slice diagonally in half. Serve.

Viennoiseries: Easy Apple Turnover

Makes 8 turnovers
Recommended serving size: 1 turnover per meal

Ingredients:

For the turnovers

1	package, 17 oz.	frozen puff pastry, thawed
4	pieces, small	baking apples, peeled, cored, diced into bite-sized pieces, pat dried with paper towel to remove excess moisture
½	cup	unwashed palm sugar, crumbled by hand to loosen granules
1	Tbsp.	almond flour
½	tsp.	cinnamon powder
-	-	all purpose flour, for

			rolling out dough
For the egg wash			
	1	piece, large	egg white, whisked in
	2	Tbsp.	water

Directions:

1. <u>To make filling</u>: combine almond flour, cinnamon powder and palm sugar until these resemble coarse meal. Toss in diced apples until well coated. Set aside.
2. On lightly floured surface, roll out puff pastry until ¼ inch thin. Slice into 8 pieces of 4" x 4" squares.
3. Divide prepared apples into 8 equal portions. Spoon on individual puff pastry squares. Fold in half diagonally. Press edges to seal.
4. Place each filled pastry on a baking tray lined with parchment paper. Make sure there is ample space in between pastries.
5. Freeze for at least 20 minutes, or until ready to bake.
6. Preheat oven to 400°F or 205°C for at 10 minutes.
7. Brush frozen pastries with egg wash. Place in hot oven, and cook for 12 to 15 minutes, or until these turn golden brown all over.
8. Remove baking tray from oven immediately. Cool slightly for easier handling.
9. Place 1 apple turnover on plate. Serve warm.

281.
Watermelon and Berry Slurry (Meal Replacement)

Makes 1 Serving

Ingredients:		
1	cup	watermelon, deseeded
½	cup	crushed ice
¼	cup	frozen blueberries
1	piece, large	frozen strawberries
1	tsp.	lime or lemon juice, freshly squeezed
¼	tsp.	green *stevia*, optional

Directions:

1. Combine all ingredients in a blender. Process until smooth. Serve immediately.

282.
Xigua and Cucumber Slurry (Meal Replacement)

Makes 1 Serving

Ingredients:

1	cup	*xigua* (golden watermelon,) deseeded (substitute any watermelon variety)
½	cup	crushed ice
1	piece, large	fresh mint leaf
½	piece	cucumber, peeled, ends removed, deseeded
¼	tsp.	green *stevia*, optional

Directions:

1. Combine all ingredients in a blender. Process until smooth. Serve immediately.

283. Yam with Coconut Butter

Makes 4 Servings
Recommended serving size: approximately 1 cup

Ingredients:		
1	piece, large	yam, unpeeled, scrubbed well
-	-	water, for boiling
-	pinch	sea salt
1	tsp., heaping	coconut butter, sugar-free (commercial blends are fine, but homemade is always better)
1½	tsp.	desiccated coconut, toasted on dry pan until golden brown and aromatic, cooled to room temperature
1	tsp.	green *stevia*

Directions:

1. Place yam in large saucepan set over high heat. Add enough water to fully submerge yam. Add pinch of salt. Put lid on. Let water come to a boil.
2. Turn down heat to lowest setting. Cook yam for 20 to 30 minutes until fork tender. Turn off heat.
3. Remove yam from saucepan. Rinse under running water. Drain.
4. Peel yam whenever possible. You can do this with your fingers or a fillet knife.
5. Place yam in a bowl, add coconut butter, and mash using a potato masher or ricer. Divide into 4 equal portions.
6. Ladle out portions using a small ice cream scooper, and place on a plate. Make small indentation in the center.
7. Combine cooled desiccated coconut and *stevia*. Divide into 4 equal portions. Sprinkle on top of yam. Serve plain or with small dollop of whipped cream.

Zucchini Bruschetta

Makes 1 Serving

Ingredients:

	slices, thick	sugar-free sourdough bread, toasted well on both sides
1	clove, large	garlic, peeled
¼	piece, small	zucchini, thinly sliced
2	tsp.	pesto (commercial blend is fine)

Directions:

1. Vigorously rub garlic clove on 1 side of each of the toasted bread slices.
2. Season zucchini slices with pesto. Toss well to combine. Divide into 2 equal portions. Spread each portion on bread slices.
3. Heat both slices in oven toaster until well heated through. Place on plate. Serve.

Chapter 4

Lunch Recipes

285.

Avocado and Steak Stuffed Pita Bread

Makes 1 Serving

Ingredients:		
1	piece, 6-inch (or smaller)	wheat/wholegrain pita bread, halved, pockets opened
1	piece, 6 oz.	minute steak (round steak or sirloin)
-	pinch	sea salt
-	dash	black pepper
-	-	olive oil, for drizzling
1	piece, small	tomato, deseeded, minced, pat-dried
1	cup	baby spinach, rinsed, spun-dried, add

¼	cup	more if desired avocado, diced into bite-sized pieces
⅛	tsp.	balsamic vinegar
¼	tsp.	English or hot mustard
1	sprig	fresh cilantro, minced
1	wedge, small	lime, fresh

Directions:

1. Marinade minute steak with salt and pepper. Lightly drizzle with olive oil.
2. Preheat stovetop or electric griller for 3 minutes, or until water sizzles when dropped on cooking surface.
3. Grill minute steak until well seared on both sides, about 2 minutes or less. Remove meat from heat immediately.
4. Place on plate. Cover with sheet of aluminum foil to rest, about 5 minutes. Julienne steak.
5. Except for lime wedge, toss remaining ingredients into small bowl. Season well with balsamic vinegar and English mustard.
6. Add in steak along with its juices. Divide in half.
7. <u>To assemble</u>: stuff equal portions of filling into each pita pocket just before serving. Squeeze lime on both. Consume immediately.

286. Broccoli and Blue Cheese Salad

Makes 1 Serving

Ingredients:

1	cup, heaping	broccoli, sliced into bite-sized florets, lightly steamed
1	cup, heaping	iceberg lettuce, rinsed, spun-dried, roughly torn, add more if desired
¼	cup	alfalfa sprouts, rinsed, spun-dried, add more if desired
½	tsp., heaping	roasted cashew nuts, lightly seasoned (do not use honey roasted ones)
1	tsp.	blue cheese
1	tsp.	sour cream

| 1 | tsp. | apple cider vinegar |
| - | - | white pepper, to taste |

Directions:

1. In a small bowl, combine blue cheese, sour cream, apple cider and white pepper. Mix until creamy.
2. In a larger bowl, add in remaining ingredients. Toss well to combine.
3. Drizzle blue cheese mix into salad just before serving. Serve.

287.

Chicken Salad on Toast

Makes 1 Serving

Ingredients:

1	slice, thick	sugar-free sourdough bread, toasted
1	leaf, large	iceberg lettuce, rinsed, spun-dried, shredded

<u>For the salad</u>

½	cup	boiled/roasted chicken meat, (leftovers are fine,) shredded or minced
1	tsp.	minced celery
1	tsp.	minced shallot
1	tsp.	cottage cheese, rinsed and drained well
¼	tsp.	mayonnaise

| - | - | sea salt and white pepper, to taste |

Directions:

1. In a bowl, combine salad ingredients. Season with salt and pepper.
2. Layer shredded lettuce leaves on toasted bread.
3. Spread chicken salad on top of leaves. Serve immediately.

288. Devilled Eggs (Mayo Free, Spicy)

Makes 1 Serving

Ingredients:		
2	pieces, small	eggs, hard-boiled, peeled, halved lengthwise, yolks and whites separated
¼	tsp.	apple cider vinegar
¼	tsp.	cottage cheese, rinsed and drained well
¼	tsp.	yellow mustard
⅛	tsp	bird's eye chili, deseeded, minced (optional)
-	-	sea salt and white mustard, to taste

| - | dash | sweet paprika powder, for garnish |
| 2 | pieces, small | sugar-free saltines |

Directions:

1. In a bowl, combine egg yolks, apple cider vinegar, cottage cheese, yellow mustard and fresh chili (if using.) Season with salt and pepper. Mix well. Divide into 4 equal portions.
2. Spoon portions into egg white cavities. Add a dash of paprika powder on top of each egg for color. Serve with saltines.

289. Endive Salad with Apples, Nuts and Cheese

Makes 1 Serving

Ingredients:		
1	head, medium	Belgian endive, halved lengthwise, cored, sliced into thick matchsticks
½	cup	arugula
½	piece, small	apple, unpeeled, cored, diced into bite-sized pieces
1	Tbsp, heaping	roasted walnuts, shelled, lightly seasoned (do not use honey-roasted)
½	tsp., heaping	gorgonzola cheese, shredded or diced
1	tsp.	balsamic vinegar

⅛	tsp.	apple cider vinegar
-	-	sea salt and white pepper, to taste

Directions:

1. In a small bowl, combine balsamic and apple cider vinegar. Season well with salt and pepper.
2. In a salad bowl. Toss rest of ingredients together. Serve immediately.

290.
Frozen Yogurt with Fruits (Meal Replacement)

Makes 12 Servings
Recommended serving size: approximately ½ cup

Ingredients:

1	tub, 32 oz.	Greek yogurt
1	piece, medium	peach, diced to bite-sized pieces
1	piece, medium	ripe mango, diced into bite-sized pieces
1	piece, medium	ripe banana, diced to bite-sized pieces
1	cup	fresh blueberries (or any berry of choice)

Directions:

1. In a large bowl, fold fruits into yogurt until just combined. Divide into 12 equal portions (approximately ½ cup.)
2. Scoop individual portions in small, freezer-safe containers (e.g. lidded aluminum cups, or silicon cups sealed with saran wrap, etc.)
3. Freeze for at least 8 hours before using. Thaw out slightly before serving.

291. Garlic Bread with Sweet Ham and Cheese

Makes 1 Serving

Ingredients:

1	piece, medium	sugar-free sourdough roll, preferably smaller than your palm, scored deeply in crisscross pattern
1	clove, small	garlic, minced
1	tsp.	butter, at room temperature
½	tsp.	fresh parsley, minced
1	Tbsp., heaping	gouda, grated
1	tsp., heaping	Asiago cheese
1	slice, thin	sweet or German ham, julienned

Directions:
1. In a bowl, combine butter, garlic, and parsley. Spread on and into sliced sides of bread.
2. Insert ham pieces into bread.

3. Top off with ham, and a few shavings of Asiago and parmesan cheese.
4. Heat bread in oven toaster until cheese is partially melted. Serve warm.

Halibut with French Beans and Peas

Makes 1 Serving

Ingredients:

1	piece, 6 oz.	halibut fillet, trimmed well
-	-	sea salt and white pepper, to taste
-	-	olive oil, for frying
1	cup, heaping	French beans, ends and strings removed, halved
½	cup	frozen peas, thawed, rinsed, drained
1	tsp.	butter
½	piece, small	lime, sliced into wedges, pips removed

Directions:

1. Lightly season fillet with salt and pepper. Pour small amount of oil into non-stick frying pan set over medium heat. Wait until oil turns smoky.
2. Fry halibut until well seared on both sides, about 3 to 5 minutes, depending on thickness of cut. Remove from pan immediately. Place on a plate and cover with sheet of aluminum foil to rest.
3. Place butter into same pan. Turn down heat to lowest setting. Add in French beans and peas. Cook until vegetables turn a shade brighter, about 3 minutes.
4. Place cooked fish on 1 side of plate, and place greens on 1 side. Add lime wedges. Squeeze lime before eating.

293.
Iceberg Lettuce Wedge Salad with Mushrooms

Makes 6 Servings
Recommended serving size: 1 wedge of lettuce, and a little under 1¼ cup of dressing

Ingredients:			
	1	head, large	iceberg lettuce, sliced into 6 equal wedges, retain core, rinsed, spun-dried
For the dressing			
	1	can, 15 oz.	button mushroom, stems and pieces, rinsed, drained well
	1	cup	Greek yogurt
	½	cup	white wine vinegar, add more if needed
	¼	cup	blue cheese or cottage cheese
	2	Tbsp.	freshly squeezed lemon juice
	½	tsp.	black pepper

| ¼ | tsp. | green *stevia* |

Directions:

1. Except for button mushrooms, combine all dressing ingredients in a bowl. Mix until creamy. If dressing is too thick, add more vinegar. Fold in mushrooms. Divide into 6 equal portions.
2. Place 1 wedge of lettuce wedge on a plate. Top with 1 portion of dressing. Serve.

294.
Jerusalem Artichoke with Quail Eggs

Makes 1 Serving

Ingredients:

4	pieces	quail eggs, hard-boiled, peeled
1	piece, small	Jerusalem artichoke, peeled, sliced into bite-sized chunks
1	piece, small	garlic clove, minced
-	-	olive oil, just enough for shallow frying
1	Tbsp.	white wine vinegar
-	-	sea salt and white pepper, to taste
½	piece, small	lime, sliced into wedges, remove pips
-	-	water, only if needed

Directions:

1. Pour small amount of oil into non-stick frying pan set over medium heat.

2. Pan-fry artichoke until golden brown on all sides. Except for the lime, add remaining ingredients into pan. Stir. Put the lid on. Cook for 20 to 25 minutes under artichokes are fork tender. Add water if pan is too dry, and artichoke is still firm. Remove from pan. Serve warm with lime wedge.

295. Kale and Almonds on *Fusilli*

Makes 1 Serving

Ingredients:

¼	cup	wholegrain *fusilli*, cooked according to package instructions, reserve
2	Tbsp.	cooking liquid
½	Tbsp.	olive oil
¼	cup	leeks, thinly sliced
1	clove, small	garlic, minced
-	-	sea salt and black pepper, to taste
1	handful, generous	fresh kale, thick stem removed, sliced into

		bite-sized pieces
½	cup	grape tomatoes, quartered
1	tsp., heaping	roasted almonds, roughly chopped
-	-	pecorino cheese, grated, for sprinkling

Directions:

1. Pour oil into saucepan set over high heat. Add in leeks and garlic. Turn down heat and sauté until leeks are soft, about 2 minutes.
2. Add in kale and tomatoes. Stir often until kale is wilted, about 4 minutes.
3. Except for cheese, add in remaining ingredients. Toss well to combine.
4. Place pasta dish on plate and sprinkle pecorino cheese on top. Serve.

285.

Lemony and Buttery Shrimp Rice

Makes 1 Serving

Ingredients:

¼	cup	wild rice, cooked according to package instructions
½	tsp.	butter, divided
¼	tsp.	olive oil
1	cup, small	raw shrimps, shelled, deveined, drained
¼	cup	frozen peas, thawed, rinsed, drained
1	Tbsp.	lemon juice, freshly squeezed
1	Tbsp.	chives, minced
-	-	sea salt, to taste

Directions:

1. Pour ¼ tsp. butter and oil into wok set over medium heat. Add in shrimps and peas. Sauté until shrimps are coral pink, about 5 to 7 minutes.
2. Add in wild rice and cook until well heated through. Season with salt and butter.
3. Transfer to a plate. Sprinkle chives and lemon juice on top. Serve.

297.
Macaroni and Chicken Fruit Cocktail Salad

Makes 2 Servings
Recommended serving size: a little less than ½ cup per person

Ingredients:		
¼	cup	cooked macaroni salad
¼	cup	roasted or boiled chicken, (leftovers are fine,) diced into bite-sized pieces
¼	cup	fruit cocktail in light syrup (canned,) drained well
2	Tbsp.	mayonnaise, low-fat
1	Tbsp.	sour cream
1	Tbsp. heaping	cottage cheese, rinsed, drained well
1	tsp.	raisins
1	tsp.	celery, minced

		sea salt and black pepper, to taste

Directions:

1. Whisk mayonnaise, sour cream, and cottage cheese until creamy.
2. Fold in remaining ingredients. Season well with salt and pepper. Chill for 1 hour before serving. This will make the raisins plump up too.
3. Divide into 2 equal portions. Serve plain or with sugar-free bread/saltines.

298.

Nectarine, Apple and Mint Cold Brew (Meal Replacement)

Makes 2 Servings

Recommended serving size: approximately 2 cups per person

Ingredients:

1	quart (4 cups)	filtered or spring water
4	teabags	white tea
1	piece, medium	apple, cored, diced into bite-sized pieces
1	piece, medium	nectarine, peeled, stone removed, diced into bite-sized pieces

Directions:

1. Combine all ingredients into large non-reactive pitcher or container. Place lid on.
2. Steep tea in fridge for 5 hours. Strain out and discard spent teabags.
3. Divide brew into 2 equal portions. Serve with apple and nectarine pieces.

299.

Olive Stuffed Kaiser Roll

Makes 1 Serving

Ingredients:		
1	piece, medium	sugar-free Kaiser roll, halved, insides scraped out to create hollow center, scraped bread minced
1	tsp.	*Fontina* or gouda cheese, shaved
1	piece, medium	pitted black olives in brine, rinsed, drained well, thinly sliced
1	piece, medium	pitted *Nicoise* olives, rinsed, drained well, thinly sliced
¼	cup	baby spinach, rinsed, spun-dried
-	pinch	black pepper, to taste

Directions:

1. Except for hollowed out Kaiser roll, combine remaining ingredients in a bowl. Toss well to combine.
2. Lightly toast both halves of Kaiser roll. Stuff bottom half with as much filling as possible. Place top half of bread. Serve.

300.

Parmesan Crusted Tilapia

Makes 1 Serving

Ingredients:

1	piece, 6 oz.	tilapia fillet, trimmed well
1	Tbsp, heaping	steel-cut oats (do not use instant,)
1	Tbsp.	parmesan cheese, grated
-	pinch	garlic powder
-	pinch	oregano powder
-	pinch	sea salt and black pepper, to taste
-	-	olive oil, for shallow frying

Directions:

1. Season fish fillet with a salt and pepper. Set aside.
2. Place remaining ingredients into blender. Process until finely milled.
3. Roll fish fillet in oatmeal mix until well coated.
4. Pour small amount of oil in non-stick frying pan, just enough to lightly grease cooking surface. Set pan over medium heat.
5. Fry tilapia until golden brown on both sides, about 3 to 5 minutes, depending on thickness of fillet. Remove from pan immediately.
6. Serve plain, with ½ cup warm wild rice, or ½ cup cooked quinoa.

301.

Quinoa with Herbs and Nuts

Makes 1 Serving

Ingredients:

1	piece, 6 oz.	tilapia fillet, trimmed well
1	Tbsp, heaping	steel-cut oats (do not use instant,)
1	Tbsp.	parmesan cheese, grated
-	pinch	garlic powder
-	pinch	oregano powder
-	pinch	sea salt and black pepper, to taste
-	-	olive oil, for shallow frying

Directions:

1. Season fish fillet with a salt and pepper. Set aside.
2. Place remaining ingredients into blender. Process until finely milled.
3. Roll fish fillet in oatmeal mix until well coated.
4. Pour small amount of oil in non-stick frying pan, just enough to lightly grease cooking surface. Set pan over medium heat.
5. Fry tilapia until golden brown on both sides, about 3 to 5 minutes, depending on thickness of fillet. Remove from pan immediately.
6. Serve plain, with ½ cup warm wild rice, or ½ cup cooked quinoa.

302.

Reuben Sandwich (Low Fat)

Makes 1 Serving

Ingredients:		
2	slices, thin	sugar-free rye bread
1	slice, thick	corned beef, deli-sliced, warmed
1	slice, thin	Swiss cheese
¼	tsp.	Italian vinaigrette, preferably homemade, but low-sodium commercial blend is okay
⅛	tsp.	Butter
¼	cup	traditional sauerkraut, drained well, preferably homemade, but low-sodium commercial blend is okay, add more if desired

Directions:

1. Spread butter on 1 slice of bread, and Italian vinaigrette on the other.
2. Stack corned beef, Swiss cheese and sauerkraut on buttered slice.
3. Top everything off with remaining slice of bread. Halve diagonally. Serve.

303. Smoked Salmon and Herbed Cream Cheese Sandwich

Makes 1 Serving

Ingredients:

2	slices, thin	sugar-free sourdough bread, toasted
4	slices, thin	smoked salmon
2	tsp., level	cream cheese, at room temperature
1	stalk, thin	chive, minced
2	leaves, small	parsley, minced

Directions:

1. Combine cream cheese, chives and parsley in a small bowl. Spread this equally on both bread slices.
2. Sandwich smoked salmon in between. Serve.

304. Three-Cheese Salad on Fresh Greens

Makes 1 Serving

Ingredients:		
2	balls, small	buffalo mozzarella, drained, quartered
1	tsp.	grated edam cheese, or any hard cheese of choice
1	tsp.	cottage cheese, rinse, drained
1	tsp.	apple cider vinegar, add more if desired
1	head	iceberg lettuce, rinsed, spun-dried, chopped into bite-sized pieces
1	piece, small	fresh *jalapeño* pepper,

1	piece, medium	deseeded, julienned unripe tomato, sliced int bite-sized pieces
1	stalk	parsley, roughly torn

Directions:

1. Toss all ingredients in large salad bowl. Season well with apple cider vinegar. Serve immediately.

Uccelli Scappati (Rolled Veal)

305.

Makes 1 Serving

Ingredients:

2	pieces, approx. 6 oz.	veal tenderloin, sliced thinly slightly larger than the size of your palm (ask your butcher to do this for you)
2	slices, thick	*prosciutto* (ham,) julienned
2	pieces	fresh sage leaves, julienned
1	sprig	parsley, minced
4	cubes, 1" x 1"	*pancetta* (bacon)
1/8	tsp.	olive oil

Additional Equipment: 2 short toothpicks or skewers that will fit inside a frying pan.

Directions:

1. Place veal tenderloin on chopping board. Cover with saran wrap. Pound into even thickness using a meat mallet. Remove saran wrap.
2. Layer a slice on ham and sage leaf on top of each. Divide equal portions of parsley on top each. Roll tightly. Divide each into quarters, or roughly the size of the *pancetta*.
3. Skewer 1 piece of bacon on each stick. Skewer quartered pieces of rolled veal. Skewer remaining bacon cube for last.
4. Place oil in non-stick frying pan set over medium heat.
5. Fry skewered meat on sticks until well seared on both sides, about 3 to 5 minutes.
6. Removed from pan immediately. Place on a plate. Tent with aluminum foil to rest for 5 minutes.
7. Serve on plate, either plain or with couscous or polenta. This can also be served on a bed of fresh greens.

Valencia Salad (*Ensalada Valencia*)

Makes 1 Serving

Ingredients:		
1	head, small	Romaine lettuce, rinsed, spun-dried, sliced into bite-sized pieces
½	piece, small	shallot, julienned
½	piece, small	satsuma or tangerine, pulp only
1	tsp., heaping	Kalamata or Sicilian olives in oil, pitted, drained lightly, halved, julienned
1	tsp.	white wine vinegar
1	tsp.	Dijon or yellow mustard
1	tsp.	extra virgin olive oil

⅛	tsp.	honey (optional)
1	pinch	fresh thyme, minced
-	-	sea salt and black pepper, to taste

Directions:

1. Combine vinegar, oil, fresh thyme, salt, mustard, black pepper, and honey (if using.) Whisk well until dressing emulsifies a little.
2. Toss together remaining salad ingredients in salad bowl.
3. Drizzle dressing on top when about to serve. Serve immediately with 1 slice if sugar-free sourdough bread or saltine.

307.
Watercress Salad with Cucumbers and Smoked Salmon

Makes 1 Serving

Ingredients:

1	bunch, large	watercress, roots removed, rinsed, drained, add more if needed
1	piece, 4 oz.	smoked salmon
2	pieces, small	red grape tomato, quartered

For cucumber vinaigrette:

½	piece, small	cucumber, unpeeled, halved, deseeded, thinly sliced
1	Tbsp.	white wine vinegar
¼	tsp.	extra virgin olive oil
⅛	tsp.	sugar

-	-	sea salt and black pepper, to taste
½	Tbsp.	fresh dill, reserve a pinch for garnish

For creamy dressing:

2	pieces, large	*calamondin* juice, freshly squeezed, pips removed
1	Tbsp.	*crème fraiche*
¼	Tbsp.	wasabi or prepared horseradish
¼	Tbsp.	English or grainy mustard

Directions:

1. Except for cucumbers, combine ingredients of vinaigrette in a large mixing bowl. Add in cucumbers, and let steep for 2 minutes.
2. In another bowl, whisk ingredients of creamy dressing until mix emulsifies.
3. To assemble: place watercress on plate. Drizzle with half portions of creamy dressing.

4. Drape smoked salmon pieces on top. Dot with quartered tomatoes.
5. Using a slotted spoon, fish out cucumbers from vinaigrette. Place on top of salad. You can serve this as is. Or if preferred, serve vinaigrette and/or creamy dressing on the side.

Xacuti

Makes 1 Serving

Ingredients:		
2	pieces, medium	chicken thigh fillets, rinsed, pat-dried, diced into bite-sized pieces
-	-	sea salt, to taste
1	tsp.	grape seed oil
½	piece, small	shallot, minced
	Tbsp.	coconut cream
¼	tsp.	tomato paste
-	-	water, for boiling
<u>For the *xacuti masala*</u> (make this in advance, keep leftovers for other dishes)		
2	Tbsp.	coriander seeds, raw
1	Tbsp.	cumin seeds, raw

1	Tbsp.	fennel seeds, raw
1	Tbsp.	garlic powder
1	Tbsp.	ginger powder
1	Tbsp.	roasted shelled peanuts, unsalted
1	Tbsp.	sesame seeds, raw
½	Tbsp.	poppy seeds, raw
1	tsp.	cloves, whole
1	tsp.	black peppercorns
1	tsp.	red pepper flakes
½	tsp.	ground turmeric powder
½	tsp.	turmeric powder
6	pieces, medium	banana chili
1	piece, 2-inch long	cinnamon stick

Garnish, all optional

1	sprig	cilantro, minced
¼	wedge, small	lime

Directions:

1. <u>To prepare *xacuti masala*</u>: place all ingredients on a dry pan set over low heat. Gently stir-fry spices until brown and aromatic. Do not burn.
2. Remove from pan, and let cool to room temperature before processing.
3. Place ingredients in a spice blender. Process until powdery. Place in airtight container until ready to use. For this recipe, you only need ¼ heaping teaspoon.

4. <u>To cook chicken</u>: lightly season chicken thigh fillets with salt.
5. Pour oil in wok set over medium heat. Add in shallots. Cook until limp and transparent, about 2 minutes.
6. Add in chicken. Stir-fry until meat is seared on all sides. Add just enough water to submerge chicken. Let water come to a full boil. Put lid on. Turn down heat. Simmer until chicken is fork tender, or 20 to 25 minutes. Water should be reduced by half by this time.
7. Add in tomato paste, coconut cream and ¼ teaspoon of *xacuti masala*. Mix.
8. Cook until *masala* thickens.

9. <u>To assemble</u>: place dish on plate. Sprinkle cilantro leaves on top, if using. Serve with wedge of lime. You can also serve this with ½ cup wild rice, or brown rice.

309.

Yang Chow

Makes 1 Serving

Ingredients:

½	cup	cooked brown or red rice, forked through to loosen grains
1	stalk, large	leek, minced, reserve pinch for garnish
⅛	tsp.	coconut or palm oil
⅛	tsp.	garlic powder
¼	cup	frozen shrimps, thawed, rinsed, drained
1	Tbsp., heaping	frozen peas, thawed, rinsed, drained
1	piece, small	egg, whisked
1	piece, large	cabbage leaf, tough stem removed, julienned

		sea salt, and white pepper to taste

Directions:

1. Place oil in wok set over medium heat. Wait for oil to turn slightly smoky.
2. Add in chives and stir fry until wilted, about 1 minute.
3. Add in cabbage, peas and shrimps. Cook until heated through, about 2 minutes.
4. Add in remaining ingredients. Cook until egg is done, while breaking larger clumps of rice. Season with salt and pepper.
5. Remove fried rice from wok. Sprinkle pinch of fresh leeks on top. Serve warm.

310.

Zesty Pork Tenderloin with Wild Rice

Makes 1 Serving

Ingredients:

½		cup fresh cooked brown or red rice
1	piece, 6 oz.	pork chop, deboned, skin removed
2	Tbsp.	white wine vinegar
1	tsp.	garlic powder
¼	tsp.	coconut oil
-	-	sea salt and white pepper, to taste

Directions:

1. Using meat mallet, tenderize pork chop for about 30 seconds. Snip edges of meat to prevent curling. Marinade with garlic powder, vinegar and pepper for at least 30 minutes before cooking. Drain well. Discard marinade.
2. Pour oil in small non-stick frying pan set over medium heat. Wait for oil to turn slightly smoky before frying pork chop. Cook meat until golden brown on both sides, about 4 to 5 minutes. Remove from pan and cover with aluminum foil.
3. Place rested pork chop on plate. Season with salt. Serve warm with rice.

Chapter 5

Dinner in 6 Steps (or Fewer)

310.

Acquacotta (Slow Cooker Recipe)

Makes 4 Servings, freeze excess for later use, microwave to reheat
Recommended portion size: a little over 1 cup

Ingredients:		
1	tsp.	garlic powder
1	tsp.	onion powder
1	tsp.	thyme powder or dried thyme
1	can, 15 oz.	diced tomatoes
1	can, 15 oz.	button mushrooms, whole, rinsed drained well, quartered
1	piece, 6 oz.	chicken thigh fillet, diced
4	slices, thick	wholegrain or coarse grained, sugar-free bread, cubed

		into bite-sized pieces
4	cups	chicken or vegetable stock, low-sodium, low fat
-	-	sea salt and white pepper, to taste
1	stalk, large	parsley, minced, for garnish
-	-	Parmigiano-Reggiano, grated, for garnish

Directions:

1. Except for garnishes and bread, place all ingredients in large crock pot set on highest setting.
2. Turn down heat to medium setting after an hour. Let stew simmer for 4 to 5 hours undisturbed. Turn off heat.
3. Stir in bread. Let stew sit undisturbed for at least 5 minutes.
4. <u>To serve</u>: divide stew into 4 equal portions. Serve into individual bowls. Sprinkle small amounts of cheese and parsley on top. Serve warm.

311.
Beef Bourguignon

Makes 4 Servings, freeze excess for later use, microwave to reheat

Recommended portion size: a little over 1 cup

Ingredients:		
2	pounds	beef chuck roast, cut into 1-inch cubes, pat dried to remove excess moisture
½	tsp.	sea salt or kosher salt
¼	tsp.	white pepper
1	tsp.	olive oil
2	cloves, large	garlic, minced
1	piece, large	onion, roughly chopped
1	piece, large	carrots, cubed into 1-inch cubes
1	piece, large	dried bay leaf, whole
1	bottle, 750 ml.	dry red wine
2	cups	beef broth, low-sodium, low–fat

1	tsp.	fresh thyme, roughly chopped
1	piece, small	lemon, sliced into wedges, remove pips

Directions:

1. Pour oil into oven-safe Dutch oven set over medium heat.
2. Vigorously rub salt and white pepper into cubed beef chuck. Fry these in heated oil until well seared or golden brown on all sides. Cook beef in batches so as not to overcrowd pan. Transfer partially cooked meat on plates.
3. In same Dutch oven, add in onions and carrots. Sauté until former is limp and transparent, about 1 minute. Add in remaining ingredients into Dutch oven, including beef cubes. Stir gently. Secure lid. Turn off heat.
4. Preheat oven to 300°F or 150°C for at least 10 minutes.
5. Place cookware into oven. Slow cook stew for 4 hours. Remove from oven.
6. Divide into 4 equal portions. Serve into individual bowls. Serve with lemon wedge. Squeeze juice into stew before eating. Serve warm.

312. Chili: Meaty, Spicy, Speedy (Slow Cooker Recipe)

Makes 6 Servings, freeze excess for later use, microwave to reheat

Recommended portion size: ¾ cup

Ingredients:		
1	pound	90% to 95% lean ground beef, crumbled
3	links, large	Italian sausage, casings removed, meat crumbled
2	cans, 15 oz. each	diced tomatoes, roughly chopped
1	can, 15 oz.	chickpeas, rinsed, drained well
1	can, 15 oz.	cannelloni beans, rinsed, drained well
1	cup	vegetable broth or chicken broth, low-

		sodium, low-fat
1	piece, large	bird's eye chili, minced
1	Tbsp.	tomato paste
1	tsp.	red pepper flakes
1	tsp.	onion powder
½	tsp.	chili powder
½	tsp.	cumin powder
½	tsp.	paprika powder
¼	tsp.	oregano powder
-	-	sea salt and black pepper to taste

Directions:

1. Pour ingredients into crock pot set on medium heat. Mix once. Secure lid.
2. Let chili cook for 3 to 4 hours undisturbed. Taste. Adjust seasoning. Mix well. Break larger clumps of meat, if any.
3. Turn off heat. Divide chili into 6 equal portions. Ladle into individual bowls. Consume as is, or with sugar-free toasted tortillas.

313. Daikon, Pork and Taro in Stewed Tamarind (Slow Cooker Recipe)

Makes 4 Servings, freeze excess for later use, microwave to reheat

Recommended portion size: 1½ cups

Ingredients:		
3	cup	water
2	pieces, large	ripe tomatoes, quartered
1	piece, large	onion, roughly chopped
1	piece, large	Manila tamarind, unripe, scrubbed
1	piece, large	*daikon*, peeled, cubed
1	piece, large	taro, peeled, cubed
½	pound	pork shoulder, sliced into bite-sized cubes
1	tsp., heaping	tamarind paste
1	tsp.	fish sauce

½	tsp.	black peppercorns

Directions:

1. Except tamarind paste, pour ingredients into crock pot set on medium heat. Mix. Secure lid. Let stew cook for hours undisturbed. Mix in tamarind paste.
2. Turn off heat. Divide stew into 4 equal portions. Ladle into individual bowls. Consume as is, or with rice.

314.
Egg Drop Soup with Straw Mushrooms

Makes 4 Servings, freeze excess for later use, microwave to reheat

Recommended portion size: 1 cup

Ingredients:		
2	pieces, small	eggs, whisked well
4	cups	vegetable or beef broth, low-sodium, low-fat
1	can, 15 oz.	straw mushroom, rinsed, drained well, roughly chopped
1	stalk, large	leek, minced
1	piece, 1-inch long	ginger, peeled, grated
1	Tbsp., heaping	cornstarch, dissolved in
2	Tbsp.	water
1	tsp.	dark soy sauce

Directions:

1. Except for eggs, pour ingredients into pot set on medium heat. Secure lid.
2. Let soup come to a boil. Turn down heat to lowest setting. Pour egg into soup in thin streams. Gently mix. Turn off heat. Ladle into individual cups. Serve warm.

315.

Fennel, Caper and Peas on Baked Snapper

Makes 1 Serving

Ingredients:

1	fillet	snapper fillet, trimmed well
1	stalk	fresh cilantro, minced
-	pinch	smoky paprika
-	pinch	sea salt

For the toppings

½	cup	frozen peas, thawed, blanched, drained
½	cup	fennel bulb, thinly shaved using mandolin or vegetable peeler
¼	tsp.	capers in brine, rinsed, drained well

¼	tsp.	balsamic vinegar
⅛	tsp.	dried pepper flakes
1	tsp.	lemon, freshly juiced
	-	sea salt

Directions:

1. <u>To make toppings</u>: toss ingredients into large bowl. Set aside.
2. <u>To prepare fish</u>: preheat oven to 450°F or 230°C for at least 5 minutes. Line a baking sheet with parchment paper. Lightly season fish fillet.
3. Place on prepared baking sheet. Bake for 10 minutes. Remove from oven.
4. Sprinkle toppings on fish fillet. Bake for another 10 minutes.
5. Carefully remove fish fillet and plate. Serve warm.

316.

Grapes and Stir-Fried Pork Tenderloin

Makes 1 Serving

Ingredients:

1	medallion, 6 oz.	pork tenderloin, trimmed well, remove membrane
-	-	sea salt
-	drop	sesame oil
For grape vinaigrette		
¼	cup	green grapes, quartered, remove seeds
¼	cup	red grapes, quartered, remove seeds
1	tsp.	apple cider vinegar, freshly juiced
-	-	black peppercorns, freshly cracked

Directions:

1. <u>To make vinaigrette</u>: toss ingredients in a bowl. Chill prior to serving.

2. <u>To prepare pork</u>: preheat stovetop or electric grill for at least 3 minutes.
3. Lightly season pork with salt and sesame oil. Grill only until well seared on both sides, about 10 to 12 minutes. Remove from grill. Tent with aluminum foil, and allow meat to rest 5 minutes.
4. Place cooked pork medallion on plate. Top off with vinaigrette. Serve.

317.

Hot Halibut with Pineapples and Peppers

Makes 1 Serving

Ingredients:

1	piece, 6 oz.	halibut fillet, trimmed well
-	-	sea salt
1	Tbsp., heaping	almond flour
1/8	tsp.	coconut oil, for frying

For sauce

1	can, 8 oz,	pineapple tidbits in light syrup
1	piece, large	banana chili, halved, deseeded, minced
1/4	piece, small	red bell pepper, julienned
1	tsp.	tomato paste

Directions:

1. To prepare fish: pour oil in non-stick frying pan set over medium heat.
2. Season halibut with salt. Dredge in almond flour until well coated. Fry until golden crisp on both sides. Transfer cooked fish to a plate.
3. In the same pan, pour in sauce ingredients. Mix gently. Cook until thickened, about 2 minutes. Pour sauce on top of fish. Serve warm.

318.

Inferno Chicken-Ginger Stew

Makes 1 Serving

Ingredients:

1	cup	chicken broth, low-sodium, low-fat
1	cup	water
¼	cup	chicken thigh fillet, diced
¼	cup	cooked egg noodles
1	tsp.	fish sauce
-	dash	white pepper
-	dash	garlic powder, add more if desired
-	dash	onion powder
1	piece, small	bird's eye chili, minced
1	piece, 1-inch medallion	ginger, peeled, crushed
1	piece, small	unripe papaya, peeled, diced

Directions:
1. Place all ingredients in large Dutch oven set over high heat. Let liquid come to a full boil. Turn down heat to lowest setting. Put lid on. Let stew cook for 20 minutes, or until papaya is fork tender. Turn off heat. Consume as is, or with ½ cup of cooked rice. Serve warm.

319.

Jalapeño Chicken Fillets

Makes 1 Serving

Ingredients:		
2	pieces, medium	chicken thigh fillets, rinsed, pat-dried, pounded level using meat mallet
2	pieces, large	whole jalapeno peppers, fresh, stemmed
2	Tbsp.	cheddar cheese, grated, divided
-	-	sea salt and white pepper to taste
1	tsp., heaping	white flour
1	piece, small	egg, whisked well
1	tsp., heaping	sugar-free breadcrumbs
-	-	coconut oil, for frying

Directions:

1. Lightly grease non-stick frying pan with oil. Set over medium heat.
2. Lightly season chicken fillets with salt and pepper. Sprinkle equal portion of cheese on each, and top off with jalapeño apiece. Roll fillets tightly, tucking sides in to prevent cheese from spilling out. Secure edges with toothpicks.
3. Roll fillets in flour first, then egg, and then breadcrumbs. Shallow fry until golden on all sides. Remove from pan. Drain excess grease on paper towels. Serve warm.

321. Kick Ass Cheesy Beef and Mushroom Slider

Makes 1 Serving

Ingredients:

1	medallion, 6 oz.	beef tenderloin, trimmed well, remove membrane
-	-	sea salt and white pepper, to taste
⅛	tsp.	butter
⅛	tsp.	olive oil, for frying
1	piece, small	shallot, thinly sliced
1	piece, large	fresh button mushroom, thinly sliced
1	piece, small	sugar free Kaiser roll, halved, lightly toast cut sides
1	tsp. level	blue cheese

Directions:

1. Lightly season beef medallion with salt and pepper. Set aside.
2. Place oil and butter in shallow frying pan set over medium heat.

3. Cook shallots until limp and transparent, about 1 minute. Using slotted spoon, remove shallots to a plate. Cook mushrooms in same pan until browned. Remove to a plate.
4. Cook beef medallion on same pan, until seared well on all sides, turning often. Remove to a plate. Tent with aluminum foil to rest for 5 minutes.
5. <u>To assemble</u>: stack shallots, beef medallion and mushrooms on bottom half of Kaiser roll. Spread blue cheese on cut side of remaining bread slice. Place on top of burger. Consume as is, or with bed of undressed salad greens. Serve.

322.

Laing (Taro Leaves in Coconut Sauce, Slow Cooker Recipe)

Makes 4 Servings

Recommended serving size: ½ cup cooked taro leaves, serve with ½ cup cooked rice

Ingredients:		
4	cups, heaping	dried taro leaves
¼	cup	ground pork, about 85% to 90% lean
2	cans, 15 oz.	coconut cream, divided
1	tsp.	shrimp paste (substitute high quality fish sauce, if desired)
1	piece, small	bird's eye chili, minced

Directions:

1. Except for 1 can of coconut cream, place all ingredients in crock pot set at medium setting. Secure lid. Cook undisturbed for 3 to 3½ hours.
2. Pour remaining can of coconut cream before turning off heat. Stir and serve.

323.
Mushroom Stew (Slow Cooker Recipe, Vegan)

Makes 4 Servings
Recommended serving size: 1 cup

Ingredients:		
3½	cups	vegetable broth, low-sodium, low-fat
1	cup	dried *shiitake* mushrooms, soaked in water for at least 3 hours, stems trimmed, quartered, reserve
½	cup	mushroom soaking liquid
1	can, 15 oz.	button mushrooms, whole, rinsed, drained well, quartered
1	piece, small	carrot, diced into bite-sized pieces
1	piece, small	sweet potato, diced into

1	tsp.	bite-sized pieces
1	tsp.	garlic powder
1	tsp.	onion powder
1	tsp.	oregano powder
1	tsp.	sea salt
1	tsp.	white pepper
1	tsp.	tomato paste

Directions:
1. Place all ingredients in crock pot set at medium setting. Secure lid. Cook undisturbed for 4 to 4½ hours. Serve with couscous or polenta. Serve warm.

Nimbu Rice: Spiced Rice with Cashew and Chili (Vegan)

Makes 1 Serving

Ingredients:		
½	cup	cooked brown or wild, forked through
1	piece, large	jalapeño pepper, stemmed, minced
1	stalk, large	leeks, minced, reserve pinch for garnish
1	tsp., heaping	roasted cashew nut, unseasoned, roughly chopped
1	tsp., heaping	frozen peas, thawed, drained well
⅛	tsp.	olive oil
-	dash	turmeric powder
-	-	sea salt or black pepper to taste

Directions:

1. Pour oil in wok set over high heat. Sauté leeks until soft, about 1 minute.
2. Add in remaining ingredients. Stir-fry until rice and peas are warmed through, about 3 minutes. Season lightly. Garnish with pinch of leeks. Serve warm.

325.
Olive and Cheese Bruschetta with Smoked Salmon

Makes 1 Serving

Ingredients:		
4	strips, large	smoked salmon
2	slices, thick	sugar-free sourdough bread, toasted well on both sides
1	clove, large	garlic, peeled
2	tsp.	*Kalamata* olives, pitted, minced, reserve
1	tsp.	olive oil (from *Kalamata*)
1	tsp.	cottage cheese, rinsed, drained well

Directions:
1. Vigorously rub garlic clove on 1 side of each of the toasted bread slices.
2. Spread equal portions of cottage cheese and minced olives on garlic side of bread. Layer 2 slices of salmon on each slice, and drizzle olive oil on top.
3. Pop both slices into oven toaster, and cook until well heated through.
4. Place bruschetta on plate. Serve warm.

326. Prawns in Buttery Garlic Rice

Makes 1 Serving

Ingredients:

½	cup	cooked brown or wild, forked through
¼	cup	frozen peas, thawed, drained well
4	pieces, large	tiger prawns, shelled, deveined, halved lengthwise, (substitute ¾ cup frozen shrimps, thawed, drained well)
1	clove, large	garlic, minced
⅛	tsp.	butter
⅛	tsp.	olive oil
-	-	sea salt

Directions:

1. Pour oil in wok set over high heat. Sauté butter until golden and aromatic. Do not burn. Remove from wok immediately.

2. In same wok, stir-fry prawns until these turn coral, about 3 minutes. Season well.
3. Add in remaining ingredients, including garlic. Cook until rice and peas are heated through, about 3 more minutes. Serve warm.

327.

Quaglie con Pancetta (Quail Wrapped Pancetta)

Makes 1 Serving

Ingredients:

1	piece, medium	quail, ask your butcher to prepare and truss this for baking
4	strips, thin	pancetta
1	stalk, small	fresh rosemary, lightly bruised with dull edge of knife
1/8	tsp.	balsamic vinegar
1/8	tsp.	olive oil
1/2	piece, small	lime, sliced into small wedges, pips removed, divided
-	-	sea salt and black pepper, to taste

Directions:

1. Preheat oven to 375°F or 190°C for at least 15 minutes. Line a small baking dish (just enough for 1 quail) with parchment paper. Set aside.

2. Vigorously rub rosemary all over quail. Stuff leftover herb into quail cavity, along with half portion of lime wedges.
3. Lightly season bird with salt and pepper. Drizzle balsamic vinegar and oil on top.
4. Place quail into baking dish. Drape pancetta strips on top of bird.
5. Place a sheet of aluminum foil, and bake for 30 minutes. Remove aluminum foil, and cook for another 15 to 30 minutes, until pancetta turns golden brown.
6. Serve with remaining lime wedges.

328.
Ragu with Lentils (Slow Cooker Recipe)

Makes 1 Serving

Ingredients:		
1	can, 15 oz.	diced tomatoes
1	cup	vegetable broth, low-sodium, low-fat
¼	cup	ground beef, 90% lean, crumbled well
¼	cup	dried green lentils
⅛	tsp.	dried basil
⅛	tsp.	dried oregano
⅛	tsp.	garlic powder
⅛	tsp.	onion powder
-	-	sea salt and black pepper, to taste

Directions:
1. Pour all ingredients in large crock pot set on medium setting. Mix. Secure lid. Cook undisturbed for 4 hours. Adjust seasoning if needed. Serve warm.

328.

Sopas (Creamy Soup, Slow Cooker Recipe)

Makes 1 Serving

Ingredients:

½	cup	cooked elbow macaroni
1	cup	milk or any non-dairy substitute
1	cup	vegetable broth, low-sodium, low-fat
1	piece, small	chicken thigh fillet, minced
1	piece, small	carrot, diced
¼	cup	red bell pepper, diced
⅛	tsp.	garlic powder
⅛	tsp.	onion powder
-	-	sea salt and black pepper, to taste

Directions:
1. Except for cooked pasta and milk, pour all ingredients in large crock pot set on medium setting. Mix. Secure lid. Cook undisturbed for 4 hours. Turn off heat.
2. Add macaroni and milk just before serving.

329.

Tangy Sugar-Free Cola Chicken

Makes 4 Servings
Recommended serving size: quarter chicken per person

Ingredients:		
1	piece, 2½ to 3 lb.	chicken, giblets removed, pat-dried inside out
1	can, 12 oz.	sugar-free cola, divided
1	Tbsp.	Dijon or yellow mustard
1	Tbsp.	white wine vinegar
1	tsp.	soy sauce
1	piece, large	white onion, quartered
-	pinch	black pepper, add more if desired

Directions:

1. Preheat oven to 375°F or 190°C for at least 15 minutes. Line a deep baking dish with parchment paper. Set aside.
2. In a small bowl, combine half of cola, mustard, vinegar, soy sauce and black pepper. Using pastry brush, generously season chicken inside out. Reserve leftover mix for basting.

3. Place can (with remaining cola) in center of baking dish. Place chicken on top. The can should be nestled inside chicken cavity. Strew onions around base of chicken. Bake for 45 to 50 minutes, basting often.
4. Carefully remove chicken from its cola seat. Rest for 15 minutes. Quarter. Serve.

330. *Urta con Verduras:* Bream with Vegetables

Makes 1 Serving

Ingredients:

1	piece, 6 oz.	bream fillet, trimmed well
1	piece, large	tomato, deseeded, thinly sliced
1	piece, large	onion, thinly sliced
¼	cup	green bell pepper, thinly sliced
¼	cup	potato, unpeeled, halved, thinly sliced
¼	cup	cooking sherry
-	-	sea salt and white pepper, to taste

Directions:

1. Preheat oven to 375°F or 190°C for at least 15 minutes. Line a small baking dish with parchment paper. Set aside. Lightly season fish fillet with salt and pepper.
2. In a small bowl, combine tomatoes, onion, bell pepper, potatoes, and sherry. Divide into 2 equal portions. Place half portion in prepared baking dish.

3. Place fish fillet on top, then add in remaining vegetables to cover fish.
4. Bake for 20 to 25 minutes, until potatoes are cooked. Remove from oven. Rest for 5 minutes. Serve warm.

331. Vegetable, Chicken and Mushroom Pot Pie

Makes 1 Serving

Ingredients:

| 1 | package, 17 oz. | puff pastry dough, cut into 10-inch square, rolled thin, frozen pastry is best |

For the filling

1/4	cup	cooked chicken, shredded, leftovers are best
1/4	cup	carrots, diced
1/4	cup	frozen peas, thawed, drained well
1/2	cup	vegetable broth, low-sodium, low-fat
1	can, 4 oz.	button mushrooms, pieces and stems, rinsed, drained

| 2 | Tbsp. | whole fat milk |
| - | - | sea salt and black pepper, to taste |

Directions:

1. Preheat oven to 400°F or 205°C for at least 15 minutes. Except pastry, combine ingredients in large (enough) ramekin, about 6 to 8 oz. Drape puff pastry dough on top. Seal edges using fork tines. Trim off excess dough.
2. Bake for 15 to 20 minutes until pastry turns brown. Remove from oven. Serve.

332. Waldorf Salad with Cashew Nuts

Makes 1 Serving

Ingredients:		
1	cup, loosely packed	arugula leaves, add more if desired
1	cup, loosely packed	iceberg lettuce, shredded, add more if desired
¼	cup	apple, diced
¼	cup	cooked chicken, shredded, leftovers are best
¼	cup	seedless grapes, halved
1	tsp., heaping	roasted cashew nut, lightly seasoned
1	tsp.	blue cheese
1	tsp.	Greek yogurt
1	tsp.	lemon juice, freshly squeezed, add

		more if needed
-	-	black pepper, to taste

Directions:

1. In a small bowl, whisk blue cheese, Greek yogurt, lemon juice and black pepper until creamy. If dressing is too thick, add more lemon juice.
2. In a large bowl, toss to combine remaining salad ingredients.
3. Drizzle in dressing just before serving.

333.
Xia (Shrimps) Tangerine Stew with Swamp Cabbage

Makes 1 Serving

Ingredients:

2	cups	water, for boiling
1	cup, heaping	large shrimps, peeled
¼	tsp., heaping	tamarind paste
2	pieces, large	tomatoes, quartered
1	piece, small	fresh tamarind
1	piece, small	shallot, quartered
1	bundle, generous	swamp cabbage tops and tender stems only, sliced into 2-inch long slivers
1	tsp.	fish sauce
-	-	sea salt and black pepper, to taste

Directions:
1. Except for swamp cabbage, place all ingredients into small Dutch oven set over high heat. Let water come to a full boil.
2. Add in swamp cabbage. Put lid on. Turn off heat. Rest for 1 minute. Serve warm.

334.

Yin-Yang Beef with Vegetables

Makes 1 Serving

Ingredients:

For the steak

1	piece, 6 oz.	beef sirloin steak, pounded thin using meat mallet, sliced into matchsticks
-	-	black pepper, to taste
⅛	tsp.	flour
⅛	tsp.	peanut oil
⅛	tsp.	light soy sauce

For the salad

1	piece, large	cucumber, peeled, deseeded, sliced into matchsticks
1	piece, large	radish, peeled, shaved thin using vegetable peeler

¼	tsp.	white wine vinegar
⅛	tsp.	apple cider vinegar
¼	piece, small	Asian or Mexican turnip, peeled, sliced into matchsticks
-	-	salt, to taste
1	stalk, large	leek, white part only, sliced into matchsticks

Directions:

1. <u>For the steak</u>: pour oil into non-stick frying pan set over medium heat.
2. Toss rest of steak ingredients in a bowl. Mix well. Shallow fry each matchstick until golden brown. Remove from pan. Let meat rest for 5 minutes.
3. <u>For the salad</u>: toss ingredients into salad bowl. Mix well. Season lightly.
4. <u>To assemble</u>: place salad on a plate. Top off with cooked beef steak. Serve.

335. Zesty Shrimps and Tofu with French Beans

Makes 1 Serving

Ingredients:

½	cup, loosely packed	French beans, ends and strings removed, halved diagonally
¼	cup, loosely packed	frozen shrimps
¼	cup, loosely packed	minced onions
¼	tsp.	minced garlic
⅛	tsp.	corn flour, dissolved in water
2	tsp.	water
-	-	sea salt and white pepper, to taste

For the tofu

½	cup, loosely packed	organic extra firm tofu, approximately 3 to 5 ounces, cubed, pat-dried with paper towels

1	tsp., heaping	corn flour
1/8	—	sea salt, to taste
1/8	cup	coconut oil, for shallow frying

Directions:

1. <u>For the tofu</u>: pour oil into non-stick frying pan set over medium heat.
2. Lightly season tofu with sea salt. Roll in corn flour until well coated.
3. Shallow fry cubed tofu until golden brown. Remove to a plate lined with paper towels to remove excess grease.
4. <u>For the beans</u>: discard all but ⅛ tsp. oil from pan. Add in onion and garlic. Stir-fry until onions are limp and transparent.
5. Add in remaining ingredients, including cooked tofu. Stir-fry until sauce thickens. Season lightly. Transfer to a plate. Serve warm.

Chapter 6

Cold Infusions: Snacks and Meal Replacements

336.

Black Tea with Cinnamon and Blackberries

Makes 1 quart

Recommended serving size: 1½ cups

Ingredients:		
1	quart (4 cups)	filtered or spring water
4	teabags	black tea
1	pound	fresh blackberries
1	piece, 2-inch long	cinnamon stick

Directions:

1. Place all ingredients into large pitcher. Mix while gently bruising berries. Set aside for at least 4 to 6 hours in the fridge.
2. Strain out cinnamon stick and teabags. Pour tea with berries. Always serve chilled.

337.

Black Tea with Blood Oranges and Mint

Makes 1 quart

Recommended serving size: 1½ cups

Ingredients:

1	quart (4 cups)	filtered or spring water
4	teabags	black tea
2	pieces, large	blood oranges, sliced into bite-sized wedges, pips removed
¼	cup, packed	mint or apple mint

Directions:

1. Place all ingredients into large pitcher. Mix while gently bruising fruits and herbs. Set aside for at least 4 to 6 hours in the fridge.
2. Strain out mint leaves and teabags. Pour tea with blood orange wedges. Always serve chilled.

Black Tea with Black Cherries and Lemon Balm Flowers

Makes 1 quart
Recommended serving size: 1½ cups

Ingredients:

1	quart (4 cups)	filtered or spring water
4	teabags	black tea
½	cup, heaping	fresh black cherries, pitted
1	pinch, generous	lemon balm flowers (salad-safe,) rinsed, drained
1	piece, large	lemon balm leaf, rinsed

Directions:

1. Place all ingredients into large pitcher. Mix while gently bruising berries and lemon balm leaf. Set aside for at least 4 to 6 hours in the fridge.
2. Strain out lemon balm leaf, flowers and teabags. Pour tea with cherries. Always serve chilled.

339.
Black Tea with Black Raspberries and Lavender Flowers

Makes 1 quart
Recommended serving size: 1½ cups

Ingredients:

1	quart (4 cups)	filtered or spring water
4	teabags	black tea
½	cup, heaping	fresh black raspberries
1	pinch	lavender flowers (salad-safe,) rinsed, drained

Directions:

1. Place all ingredients into large pitcher. Mix while gently bruising berries and flowers. Set aside for at least 4 to 6 hours in the fridge.
2. Strain out flowers and teabags. Pour tea with berries. Always serve chilled.

340.

Black Tea with Black Mulberries, Red Grapes and Fennel Seeds

Makes 1 quart
Recommended serving size: 1½ cups

Ingredients:

1	quart (4 cups)	filtered or spring water
4	teabags	black tea
½	cup, heaping	fresh black mulberries
½	cup, heaping	seedless red grapes, quartered
1	pinch	fennel seeds

Directions:

1. Place all ingredients into large pitcher. Mix while gently bruising berries and grapes. Set aside for at least 4 to 6 hours in the fridge.
2. Strain out seeds and teabags. Pour tea with fruits. Always serve chilled.

341.

Black Tea with Black Mulberries, Red Grapes and Fennel Seeds

Makes 1 quart
Recommended serving size: 1½ cups

Ingredients:		
1	quart (4 cups)	filtered or spring water
4	teabags	black tea
½	cup, heaping	fresh black mulberries
½	cup, heaping	seedless red grapes, quartered
1	pinch	fennel seeds

Directions:

1. Place all ingredients into large pitcher. Mix while gently bruising berries and grapes. Set aside for at least 4 to 6 hours in the fridge.
2. Strain out seeds and teabags. Pour tea with fruits. Always serve chilled.

341.

Green Tea with Basil and Strawberries

Makes 1 quart
Recommended serving size: 1½ cups

Ingredients:

1	quart (4 cups)	filtered or spring water
4	teabags	green tea
1	pound	fresh strawberries, hulled, halved
¼	cup, tightly packed	fresh basil, bruised with flat edge of knife, rinsed, drained

Directions:

1. Place all ingredients into large pitcher. Mix while gently bruising fruits and herbs. Set aside for at least 4 to 6 hours in the fridge.
2. Strain out and discard herbs and teabags. Pour green tea with fruits. Always serve chilled.

342.

Green Tea with Berries

Makes 1 quart
Recommended serving size: 1½ cups

Ingredients:		
1	quart (4 cups)	filtered or spring water
4	teabags	green tea
½	cup	frozen blueberries
½	cup	frozen strawberries, quartered
½	cup	cranberries
½	cup	seedless grapes, quartered

Directions:

1. Place all ingredients into large pitcher. Mix while gently bruising berries. Set aside for at least 4 to 6 hours in the fridge.
2. Strain out teabags. Pour green tea with berries. Always serve chilled.

343.

Green Tea with Tart Green Mangoes and Cucumbers

Makes 1 quart
Recommended serving size: 1½ cups

Ingredients:		
1	quart (4 cups)	filtered or spring water
4	teabags	green tea
1	piece, large	unripe mangoes, peeled, shaved thin using vegetable peeler
1	piece, large	cucumber, shaved thin using vegetable peeler, discard seeds

Directions:

1. Place all ingredients into large pitcher. Mix while gently bruising fruits. Set aside for at least 4 to 6 hours in the fridge.
2. Strain out teabags. Pour green tea with fruits. Always serve chilled.

344.
Green Tea with Blueberries, Lemon and Lime

Makes 1 quart
Recommended serving size: 1½ cups

Ingredients:

1	quart (4 cups)	filtered or spring water
4	teabags	green tea
½	cup, heaping	frozen blueberries
1	piece, small	lemon, sliced into bite-sized wedges
1	piece, large	lime, sliced into bite-sized wedges

Directions:

1. Place all ingredients into large pitcher. Mix while gently bruising berries and fruits. Set aside for at least 4 to 6 hours in the fridge.
2. Strain out teabags. Pour green tea with berries and fruits. Always serve chilled.

345.
Green Tea with Ripe Mango and Sweet Orange

Makes 1 quart
Recommended serving size: 1½ cups

Ingredients:		
1	quart (4 cups)	filtered or spring water
4	teabags	green tea
1	piece, large	ripe mango, flesh scooped out with fruit/ball scooper
1	piece, large	sweet orange, sliced into bite-sized wedges

Directions:
1. Place all ingredients into large pitcher. Mix while gently bruising fruits. Set aside for at least 4 to 6 hours in the fridge.
2. Strain out teabags. Pour green tea with berries and fruits. Always serve chilled.

346.

Green Tea with Citrus

Makes 1 quart
Recommended serving size: 1½ cups

Ingredients:		
1	quart (4 cups)	filtered or spring water
4	teabags	green tea
1	piece, large	blood orange, sliced into bite-sized wedges
1	piece, large	lemon, sliced into bite-sized wedges
1	piece, large	lime, sliced into bite-sized wedges
1	piece, large	sweet orange, sliced into bite-sized wedges

Directions:

1. Place all ingredients into large pitcher. Mix while gently bruising fruits. Set aside for at least 4 to 6 hours in the fridge.
2. Strain out teabags. Pour green tea with fruits. Always serve chilled.

347.

Green Tea with Fruit Seeds

Makes 1 quart
Recommended serving size: 1½ cups

Ingredients:

1	quart (4 cups)	filtered or spring water
4	teabags	green tea
1	piece, large	sweet orange, sliced into bite-sized wedges
1	piece, large	pomegranate, seeds only
1	piece, large	passion fruit, seeds only

Directions:

1. Place all ingredients into large pitcher. Mix while gently bruising orange wedges. Set aside for at least 4 to 6 hours in the fridge.
2. Strain out teabags. Pour green tea with fruits and seeds. Always serve chilled.

348.

Green Tea with Lemon and Spinach Leaves

Makes 1 quart
Recommended serving size: 1½ cups

Ingredients:		
1	quart (4 cups)	filtered or spring water
4	teabags	green tea
1	piece, large	lemon, sliced into bite-sized wedges
½	cup, tightly packed	baby spinach leaves

Directions:
1. Place all ingredients into large pitcher. Mix while gently bruising lemon wedges and spinach leaves. Set aside for at least 4 to 6 hours in the fridge.
2. Strain out leaves and teabags. Pour green tea with lemon wedges. Always serve chilled.

349.
Green Tea with Arugula Leaves, Lime, and Kale Leaves

Makes 1 quart
Recommended serving size: 1½ cups

Ingredients:

1	quart (4 cups)	filtered or spring water
4	teabags	green tea
2	pieces, large	lime, sliced into bite-sized wedges, remove pips
¼	cup, tightly packed	arugula leaves, rinsed well, drained
¼	cup, tightly packed	kale leaves, rinsed well, drained

Directions:

1. Place all ingredients into large pitcher. Mix while gently bruising lime wedges and leaves. Set aside for at least 4 to 6 hours in the fridge.
2. Strain out leaves and teabags. Pour green tea with lime wedges. Always serve chilled.

350.

White Tea with Peaches and Mint

Makes 1 quart
Recommended serving size: 1½ cups

Ingredients:		
1	quart (4 cups)	filtered or spring water
4	teabags	white tea
2	pieces, large	ripe peaches, pitted, sliced into bite-sized wedges
1	sprig, large	mint, rinsed well, drained

Directions:

1. Place all ingredients into large pitcher. Mix while gently bruising peaches and mint. Set aside for at least 4 to 6 hours in the fridge.
2. Strain out mint and teabags. Pour tea with peach wedges. Always serve chilled.

351.
White Tea with Spiced Apples and Oranges

Makes 1 quart
Recommended serving size: 1½ cups

Ingredients:		
1	quart (4 cups)	filtered or spring water
4	teabags	white tea
2	pieces, small	apples, cored, diced into bite-sized pieces
2	pieces, small	sweet oranges, diced into bite-sized pieces, remove pips
1	piece, 2-inch long	cinnamon stick

Directions:

1. Place all ingredients into large pitcher. Mix while gently bruising fruits.
2. Set aside for at least 4 to 6 hours in the fridge. Strain out cinnamon stick and teabags. Pour tea with fruits. Always serve chilled.

352.

White Tea with Apples and Watermelon

Makes 1 quart
Recommended serving size: 1½ cups

Ingredients:		
1	quart (4 cups)	filtered or spring water
4	teabags	white tea
2	cups	watermelon flesh, deseeded, cut into large cubes
2	pieces, small	apples, cored, diced into bite-sized pieces
1	sprig, large	mint

Directions:

1. Place all ingredients into large pitcher. Mix while gently bruising fruits and mint.
2. Set aside for at least 4 to 6 hours in the fridge. Strain out mint sprig and teabags. Pour tea with fruits. Always serve chilled.

353.

Satsuma Infusion

Makes 1 quart
Recommended serving size: 1½ cups

Ingredients:

1	quart (4 cups)	filtered or spring water
½	pound	Satsuma, peeled, remove pips (substitute Mandarin oranges)

Directions:

1. Place all ingredients into large pitcher. Mix while gently bruising oranges.
2. Set aside for at least an hour in the fridge. Pour drink. Consume liquid and fruits. Serve.

353.

Cilantro and Lemon Infusion

Makes 1 quart
Recommended serving size: 1½ cups

Ingredients:

1	quart (4 cups)	filtered or spring water
2	pieces, large	lemons, use pulp only
1	sprig, knotted	cilantro/coriander, rinsed well, drained

Directions:

1. Place all ingredients into large pitcher. Mix while gently bruising lemons and cilantro leaves.
2. Set aside for at least an hour in the fridge. Strain out cilantro leaves. Pour drink. Consume liquid and fruits. Serve.

354. Cilantro, Cucumber, and Lemon Infusion

Makes 1 quart
Recommended serving size: 1½ cups

Ingredients:		
1	quart (4 cups)	filtered or spring water
1	piece, large	lemons, use pulp only
1	piece, medium	cucumber, ends removed, cubed into bite-sized pieces
1	sprig, knotted	cilantro/coriander, rinsed well, drained

Directions:

1. Place all ingredients into large pitcher. Mix while gently bruising fruits.
2. Set aside for at least an hour in the fridge. Strain out cilantro leaves. Pour drink. Consume liquid and fruits. Serve.

355.

Orange Peel and Grape Infusion

Makes 1 quart
Recommended serving size: 1½ cups

Ingredients:		
1	quart (4 cups)	filtered or spring water
1	piece, large	orange peel, julienned, pulp squeezed
1	cup	seedless red grapes, quartered

Directions:

1. Place all ingredients into large pitcher. Mix while gently bruising peels and fruits.
2. Set aside for at least an hour in the fridge. Strain out orange peels. Pour drink. Consume liquid and grapes. Serve.

356.

Strawberries and Elderberry Flowers Infusion

Makes 1 quart
Recommended serving size: 1½ cups

Ingredients:

1	quart (4 cups)	filtered or spring water
1	cup	frozen strawberries, quartered
¼	cup	elderberry flowers (salad-grade,) rinsed well, drained

Directions:

1. Place all ingredients into large pitcher. Mix while gently bruising berries.
2. Set aside for at least an hour in the fridge. Strain out flowers. Pour drink. Consume liquid and berries. Serve.

357.

Apricot, Nectarine and Peach Infusion

Makes 1 quart
Recommended serving size: 1½ cups

Ingredients:

1	quart (4 cups)	filtered or spring water
1	piece, large	apricot, peeled, pitted, cubed
1	piece, large	nectarine, peeled, pitted, cubed
1	piece, large	peach, peeled, pitted, cubed

Directions:

1. Place all ingredients into large pitcher. Mix while gently bruising fruits.
2. Set aside for at least an hour in the fridge. Pour drink. Consume liquid and fruits. Serve.

358.

Large Citrus Infusion

Makes 1 quart
Recommended serving size: 1½ cups

Ingredients:		
1	quart (4 cups)	filtered or spring water
1	cup, heaping	grapefruit pulp
1	cup, heaping	*pomelo* pulp
1	cup, heaping	sweet orange pulp

Directions:

1. Place all ingredients into large pitcher. Mix while gently bruising peels and fruits.
2. Set aside for at least an hour in the fridge. Strain out orange peels. Pour drink. Consume liquid and citrus pulp. Serve.

359.

Small Citrus Infusion

Makes 1 quart
Recommended serving size: 1½ cups

Ingredients:		
1	quart (4 cups)	filtered or spring water
1	cup, heaping	ripe *calamondin* pulp
1	cup, heaping	key lime pulp
1	cup, heaping	lime pulp

Directions:

1. Place all ingredients into large pitcher. Mix while gently bruising peels and fruits.
2. Set aside for at least an hour in the fridge. Pour drink. Consume liquid and citrus pulp. Serve.

360.
Peaches and Thyme Infusion

Makes 1 quart
Recommended serving size: 1½ cups

Ingredients:

1	quart (4 cups)	filtered or spring water
2	piece, large	peaches, peeled, pitted, cubed
1	sprig, large	fresh thyme, rinsed well, drained

Directions:

1. Place all ingredients into large pitcher. Mix while gently bruising fruits and thyme.
2. Set aside for at least an hour in the fridge. Discard thyme. Pour drink. Consume liquid and fruits. Serve.

361.

Grapefruit and Rosemary Infusion

Makes 1 quart
Recommended serving size: 1½ cups

Ingredients:

1	quart (4 cups)	filtered or spring water
1	piece, medium	grapefruit pulp
1	sprig, large	fresh rosemary

Directions:

1. Place all ingredients into large pitcher. Mix while gently bruising fruits and herbs.
2. Set aside for at least an hour in the fridge. Strain out rosemary. Pour drink. Consume liquid and grapefruit pulp. Serve.

362.
Grape, Lemon, Strawberry and Thyme Infusion

Makes 1 quart
Recommended serving size: 1½ cups

Ingredients:

1	quart (4 cups)	filtered or spring water
1	cup, heaping	seedless red grapes, quartered
1	cup, heaping	strawberries, quartered
1	piece, medium	lemon, cubed
1	sprig, lagre	fresh thyme

Directions:

1. Place all ingredients into large pitcher. Mix while gently bruising fruits and herb.
2. Set aside for at least an hour in the fridge. Pour drink. Discard thyme. Consume liquid and fruits. Serve.

363.

Watermelon and Raspberry Infusion

Makes 1 quart
Recommended serving size: 1½ cups

Ingredients:		
1	quart (4 cups)	filtered or spring water
2	cups, heaping	watermelon flesh, cubed, deseeded
1	cup, heaping	raspberries

Directions:

1. Place all ingredients into large pitcher. Mix while gently bruising fruits.
2. Set aside for at least an hour in the fridge. Pour drink. Consume liquid and fruits. Serve.

364. Tropical Fruit Infusion

Makes 1 quart
Recommended serving size: 1½ cups

Ingredients:

1	quart (4 cups)	filtered or spring water
2	cups, heaping	fresh pineapple, cored, cubed
1	piece, large	ripe mango, stone removed, flesh cubed
1	piece, medium	lime, quartered

Directions:

1. Place all ingredients into large pitcher. Mix while gently bruising fruits.
2. Set aside for at least an hour in the fridge. Pour drink. Consume liquid and fruits. Serve.

365.

Blueberry, Kiwi Fruit, and Raspberry Infusion

Makes 1 quart
Recommended serving size: 1½ cups

Ingredients:

1	quart (4 cups)	filtered or spring water
1	cup, heaping	kiwi fruits, peeled, cubed
1	cup, heaping	blueberries
1	cup, heaping	raspberries

Directions:

1. Place all ingredients into large pitcher. Mix while gently bruising fruits.
2. Set aside for at least an hour in the fridge. Pour drink. Consume liquid and fruits. Serve.

Conclusion

Thank you again for downloading and reading the book, **"365 Days of Diabetic Friendly Easy to Cook Recipes."**

I hope this book gave you a better understanding on how to prepare and cook diabetic-friendly ingredients and dishes. The truth is: this kind of cooking is best done at home, where you can control portions and limit your sugar and simple carbohydrate intake. Simple dishes are the best, but that doesn't mean you have to eat raw fruits or bland, steamed vegetables all the time. There are different ways and means to get great flavors out of the plainest ingredients.

However, if you like dining out, this book lists some ingredients that you can consume safely if you do have diabetes.

The next step to take is to make these recipes your own. You can customize these according to personal taste, or if you would like to substitute local produce in your area.

Finally, if you enjoyed this book, then I'd like to ask you for a favor, would you be kind enough to leave a review for this book on Amazon? It'd be greatly appreciated!

Click here to leave a review for this book on Amazon!

Thank you once more for downloading the book. Good luck!

Check Out My Other Books

Below you'll find some of my other popular books that are popular on Amazon and Kindle as well. Simply click on the links below to check them out. Alternatively, you can visit my author page on Amazon to see other work done by me.

My Other Book –The Diabetic Cookbook- 100 Diabetic friendly Easy to Cook Recipes

My Other Book – Herbal Remedies-Herbal remedies that heal, protect and provide instant relief from Everyday Common Ailments

My Other Book –Constipation-Remedies to get rid of Chronic Constipation

My Other Book –Hemorrhoids- Natural and Herbal remedies to cure Hemorrhoids

My Other Book –Stress- Management- Best ways to handle your Stress and become Stress- Free

If the links do not work, for whatever reason, you can simply search for these titles on the Amazon website to find them.

Made in the USA
Lexington, KY
20 June 2016